NOT FOR SALE
非賣品

Growing Flowers and Foliage
for Cutting

Growing Flowers and Foliage for Cutting

Barbara Coates

Kangaroo Press

Acknowledgments

NSW Department of Agriculture.
J.H. & E.J. Williams & Sons, Murwillumbah, NSW.
Irene Edwards, Murwillumbah, NSW.
Queensland Department of Primary Industries.
Queensland Orchid Society.
Merellen Orchids, 181 Macdonnell Road, Eagle Heights, Qld.
S. Heyden, *Phalaenopsis* orchid breeder, Qld.
D. Littman, cattleya and *Dendrobium* orchid breeder, Qld.
W. Harris, *Cymbidium* orchid breeder, Qld.
J. Woolf, Toowoomba Orchid Society, Qld.
Christensen's Flowers, Brisbane Markets, Rocklea, Qld.
Tropical Blooms Pty. Ltd., Nth Qld.
Arthur Yates & Co. Pty. Ltd.

Drawings by Barbara Coates and Kim Maciuk.
Photography by Bruce Devine, Murwillumbah, NSW.

Note: Where specific companies are mentioned in this book, please note that this is not a personal recommendation but is to be used merely as a reference source.

Cover: Yarrow

First published in 1993 by Kangaroo Press Pty Ltd
3 Whitehall Road Kenthurst NSW 2156 Australia
PO Box 6125 Dural Delivery Centre NSW 2158 Australia
Typeset by G.T. Setters Pty Limited
Printed in Hong Kong by Colorcraft Ltd

ISBN 0 86417 545 0

Contents

Introduction

In Australia alone we grow over 68 million cut flowers annually. The latest Australian Bureau of Statistics figures show that 3858 hectares nationwide are used for this purpose—and this of course doesn't take into account the home gardener's efforts.

Since the beginning of civilisation, flowers and foliages have been cut for their visual appeal. Given as tokens of affection, placed on tables as decorations, used individually or *en masse*, cut flowers and foliages provide, for most people, a sense of well-being.

Have you ever been held spellbound by the beauty of just one rose? You don't have to be a flower arranging genius to appreciate the beauty of cut flowers.

But for those of us who enjoy extravaganza, just think what a wedding would be like without the flowers, or how drab a restaurant would be without at least one floral display.

As a seasoned lover and handler of cut flowers and foliages, it seems more than appropriate that I should now also be writing about them.

It is my dearest wish that we should grow even more flowers and foliages for cutting. Even though our representation on the world flower market is good, Australia still has so much more to offer, especially when considering our climate which allows us nationwide to grow an unsurpassed range of flowers and foliage species for export.

In recent years 40–60%* of exported flowers and foliages have come from Western Australia. Although Western Australia produces many European flowers their major impact on the overseas market is with Australian natives. Doesn't this percentage leave a lot of room for the rest of our states to catch up? The potential is exciting.

Whether you are an enthusiastic home gardener, florist, or someone starting or continuing a career as a commercial cut flower grower, I'm sure you will find some valuable tips in this book.

Happy reading!

The Flower Link vol. 6, no. 69

1 Know Your Garden

Whether you are a keen home gardener or commercial grower, it's important to know your soil. After all, healthy soil is the foundation to either a productive and rewarding garden or a thriving business.

Soil Preparation

Before planting your flowers or foliages, dig around the spot you wish to form into a garden. What do you find? Is the soil sandy; a friable, rich and well-drained loam; or is it sticky, hard clay?

Sandy soil

To get the best out of this soil, you will need to add plenty of humus. Humus is the word given to describe organic matter in the soil and will contain *decomposed* roots, stems, leaves and animal and insect excretions. Humus assists in the retention of water, enough for your plants' needs. Alone, sandy soil is a poor water retainer and plants dry out very quickly. Up to 100% by volume of humus can be added to your sandy soil.

Loam soil

This is the perfect soil. Loam soils are naturally well drained and hold just the correct amount of moisture for your plants' requirements.

Clay soil

Clay soil definitely needs a lot of work. A product on the market called 'Agrasol' is a bonus for really tough clay areas. By following the directions on the bottle clay is gradually turned to topsoil. The time factor involved varies according to the heaviness of the soil. But on a large scale, this could turn out to be expensive, so what else can you do?

Gypsum bought by the bag is one alternative. This can be mixed by the handful into the soil. But along with it, you will need to add plenty of humus to the soil.

To add the gypsum and humus, break up the clay either by hand or by rotary hoe to about 15 cm (6") in depth. Individual lump sizes should be no larger than a small egg. Add gypsum at a rate of 1 kg per square metre. Apply the first 500 grams, dig through the soil, then apply the remainder. Add humus as you go and fork through well. (Pinepeat is one form of humus.) The layer of humus should be approximately 10 cm (4") in depth. A small amount of coarse river sand can also be mixed through the clay, gypsum and humus. This should leave you with a rich and well-drained medium for growing plants.

Once you have determined your soil type and made any appropriate additions, for best results on level ground, garden beds should be built up somewhere between 15 cm (6") and 30 cm (12"). This will assist drainage and prevent root diseases caused by plants having 'wet feet'.

If you are building up a garden bed on top of a clay base, the previous soil preparation should still be carried out to allow maximum drainage.

After you have prepared your garden beds, mulch them to prevent water evaporation and as an aid to weed control. Straw is a good, clean type of mulch.

Acid or alkaline soil

If you are contemplating serious plant growing, you will need to know whether your soil is acid or alkaline, i.e. you will need to know its 'pH' level.

The pH scale runs from 1-14: 1 being extremely acid, 14 is extremely alkaline. The neutral point is 7. Most plants seem to grow happily in the 5.5-7.5 range but this will depend on exactly what it is you are growing. For example, gerberas grow well in a slightly acid soil pH of 5.5-6.2 while lavender prefers an alkaline soil pH of 6.5-8.0.Check your plants' requirements with your stockists.

The addition of lime to the soil will reduce acidity. To acidify soil use aluminium, iron sulphate or sulphur.

Soil pH testing kits are available from garden suppliers.

Fertilising

If you are a home gardener you will probably use one of the slow release organic fertilisers or complete plant foods which are readily available from garden suppliers.

On the other hand, if you are a commercial grower you will need to use specific formulas for feeding cut flower or foliage crops. Different formulas are required depending on what you grow and these should be supplied by the seller of your plants at the time of purchase.

It should be remembered that sometimes heavy use of fertilisers can produce a lushness to the crop which subsequently interferes with flower production. In particular, an abundance of nitro-gen can produce too many leaves and few flower heads.

Osmocote slow release fertilisers are highly recommended for providing a balanced amount of the major plant nutrients—nitrogen, phosphorus and potassium. Osmocote even have a range of products aimed at the commercial grower.

Plant production problems can also be overcome when the specific fertiliser requirements of a particular crop are met, and nutrient deficiencies and toxicities can be avoided. For example, magnesium is now recognised as a vital element for healthy flower development. Availability of this nutrient may be greatly reduced if potassium levels are too high.

The trace element boron is of particular importance to carnation growers. This also may be lacking in the soil.

The correct feeding of cut flowers is a complex business and often it is wise to contact an expert like your local nurseryman or Department of Agriculture advisor.

Following are some fertilising requirements of common plant groups.

Bulbs

The benefits of feeding your bulbs will show the following year by way of more spectacular flowers. It is a good idea to add fertiliser both during and after flowering. Use a slow release organic fertiliser for best results, otherwise a complete plant food is beneficial.

Do not remove bulb leaves before they have yellowed. Even if you fertilise your bulbs, by removing leaves too soon you will affect the flowering potential of the bulb next season.

Roses

It is preferable not to feed newly planted roses until the new spring shoots reach 5 cm (2'') in length, and then only feed sparingly. About one tablespoon of complete plant food or rose food scattered in a circle about 20 cm (8'') out from the plant's base should give good results. Lightly rake the fertiliser into the soil, cover with mulch, then water in. Approximately two cups of animal manure can be used as an alternative.

Once roses are established they can tolerate about double the amount of fertiliser recommended for new plants. Fertilise every six weeks (or follow packet directions), starting in spring when new growth is forming, through to late autumn. Do not fertilise in drought conditions.

This regime of fertilising will give you a continual supply of blooms rather than sporadic flushes of flowers.

Orchids

Feed liquid or water soluble complete fertiliser while growth is active, usually after flowering has finished. This applies particularly to warm climate orchids. Apply at a rate of half to two-thirds strength in three out of every four waterings.

Some experts advise cutting this down to one in every three waterings during the cooler, dormant periods while others don't feed their orchids at all during this time.

If parts of the orchid leaves turn yellow it could be due to a magnesium deficiency. Dolomite lime watered in every four to six months will correct this problem.

Natives

Native plants can grow quite well without being fertilised. If however you feel a fertiliser could benefit your plant, do not use one high in phosphorus.

Products on the market like Agriform tablets will feed native plants for at least 18 months with one application. When placing the plant into the soil push two or three Agriform tablets 10 cm (4'') into the hole walls making sure they are approximately 15 cm (6½'') below the ground surface so they do not come into direct contact with the roots.

Green label Osmocote, a slow release fertiliser lasting up to 9 months, can also be used to fertilise native plants.

Ferns and palms

Fish emulsion is a gentle organic fertiliser used from spring to mid-autumn, every 4–6 weeks. Follow bottle directions.

Pruning

Pruning plants can seem a frightening procedure to undertake, although in fact it is relatively easy. Most plants benefit from pruning and will indeed reward you with a display of more luxuriant leaf growth or an abundance of flowers during the following season.

Tip pruning is one of the easiest methods. Especially suitable for smaller shrubs and plants, it should be carried out once your new plant has become established in the soil. Pinch out the tips of new growth between your thumb and index finger. If tip pruning is carried out regularly the result will be a healthy, compact and dense-growing shrub which should alleviate the need for any heavier pruning in the future.

Where larger growing shrubs or trees are concerned, it is to the grower's advantage to prune these to keep them within easy reach.

For larger shrubs which have got out of hand, pruning with garden secateurs may be necessary. It is also necessary to remove spent flowers from shrubs and trees. Cut the stem on an angle just below the flower head.

If pruning away straggly foliage cut the branch down one-third of its length, no more. Pruning is always done within the foliage line, that is, cut away where there are still leaves, without cutting into the actual body of the shrub. To do this could result in the plant dying. This applies particularly to some native plants like banksias and hakeas.

The larger a hakea grows, in general the less resistant it becomes to pruning.

For most plants only prune away one-third of the growth at any one time, for hakeas, only one-quarter.

Acacias, thryptomenes and other seasonal flowering plants should be pruned immediately after flowering. This not only encourages more abundant flowering the next time round, but with acacias and thryptomenes can result in a second flowering during the one season.

Waratahs should be pruned before the flower heads have completely died so as not to interfere with new growth which rapidly appears once the flower head is spent. Prune bouvardias in late winter by cutting to one-third of their height and mulch with compost. *Limonium* 'Misty' range should be cut to ground level after flowering. Remove any dead leaves and fertilise.

Plants like grevilleas which flower for most of the year, but peak in spring, should be lightly pruned after the main flowering season. Some people prune these shrubs a few months *before* the main flowering season to encourage more blooms.

Besides pruning, to get the best out of your plants, keep them weed-free and well mulched.

Pruning roses

Why is it that the thought of rose pruning can bring about such hesitancy in us? Throw away your fears and get into it. Remove all those silver-grey dead canes at the base of the plant, making all cuts on an angle. Then start on the green stems. Count approximately 5 leaf nodules from where the rose stem shoots off the bush and cut ½ cm on an angle, preferably above an outer- rather than inner-facing eye. Cut about one-third of the bush off.

Pruning takes place at slightly different times of the year depending upon your climate. It would be foolish to prune just before the frosty season as any new growth will be burnt off. As a general guideline, rose pruning in warm, frost-free districts can be started in June or July. In other temperate areas where the frosts are occasional and the temperature mostly moderate, prune mid to late July. In colder areas leave your pruning as late as possible, say August, or in very cold areas even September.

Flushes of flowers for special occasions can be brought on by pruning again about 8–9 weeks before the event.

2 A Guide to Cut Flowers and Foliages

This chapter is aimed at getting you started as a grower, either commercially or just for pure pleasure. The following lists of exotic and native flowers, orchids and foliages will give you an idea of the species which are most suited to cutting. Unfortunately, because of their vast numbers, not all varieties within any one species could be mentioned but where possible, I've tried to pick out the most popular.

Flowering times will depend on your geographical area and climate. Stalk length may be influenced by your pruning techniques.

Key:

Feature flower	The main flower in an arrangement.
Secondary flower	The second most important flower in an arrangement.
Filler flower	Fills in between other flowers and foliages.
Outline flower	Used for making the outline of the arrangement.

Exotics

Achillea (yarrow)
Most species are flat-headed, with beaded flower heads borne on long graceful stems. Can be dried and colour dyed. Filler flower. Try 'Red the Beacon' (brick red), 'Moonshine' (lemon), or 'Cloth of Gold' (golden yellow). Flowering time is winter to late spring. Stalk length is 30–50 cm.

Agapanthus orientalis (agapanthus)
Agapanthus is available in three colours: the common rich blue, white, and the rare white flushed with blue. Masses of bell-like florets produce balls of colour. Can be used as feature or filler flower. 'Queen Fabiola' is a miniature blue-flowering agapanthus. Agapanthus flower in spring/summer. Stalk length is approximately 90 cm.

Allium (flowering onion)
Beaded white-flowering balls are borne on long straight stems. Filler or feature flower. Flowering time is late spring/early summer. Stalk length is approximately 30 cm.

Allium (flowering onion)

Alstroemeria (Peruvian lily)

A bulb which produces long stems with branching tops displaying clusters of butterfly-like flowers. It is available in a multitude of colours including deep pink, lilac, scarlet red, deep cerise pink, and yellow with an apricot tongue. Very popular cut flower. Use as secondary or feature flower. Flowers appear in late spring/summer. Stalk length is approximately 60 cm.

Anenome

A bulb plant producing a wide selection of flower colours including red, blue, rose and white. Flowers are distinguished by a black centre and are available as doubles or singles. Secondary flower. Flowering time is spring. Stalk length is approximately 30 cm.

Antirrhinum (snapdragon)

Tall straight spikes with clustered flower heads up the stem. Many colours ranging from whites, mauves, pinks through to reds and yellows. Good outline flower. Flowering time is spring/summer. Stalk length varies to approximately 30–40 cm.

Ammi majus (Queen Anne's lace)

Long stems display dainty white umbrella-like flower heads. Very popular cut flower. This species has broad parsnip-like leaves. *Daucus carrota* has a similar flower head but the leaves are lacy. Filler flower. Flowers appear in spring/summer. Stalk length is approximately 60 cm.

Anthurium andreanum (anthurium lily)

A tropical flowering lily which is available in an assortment of sizes and colours ranging from red, white and pink to the multi-coloured 'Obake' (white splashed with pink or green). Flower head is a heart-shaped spathe with a central spike (spadix). Feature flower. Flowers are produced throughout the year. Stalk length is approximately 40 cm.

Aster 'Single Rainbow'

Daisy-like flowers are borne on tall stems. Colours include white, pink, red, yellow and maroon. Available in mixed seed packets. Secondary flower. Flowering time is summer/early autumn. Stalk length is approximately 30 cm.

Aster matsumoto

Large double flower with yellow centre. Colour selections include rose pink, blue, yellow, apricot and white. Pink or blue flowers with white tips are also available. Secondary flower. Flowering time is summer/early autumn. Stalk length is approximately 30 cm.

Aster 'German Pompom'

Small double flower with yellow centre. There are nine different flower colours including blue, scarlet and white. Good filler or secondary flower. Flowering time is summer/early autumn. Stalk length is approximately 30 cm.

Aster 'Floret'

Large double flowers without any centre displayed. Colours are cream-white, pure white, cherry, pink, mauve and purple. Secondary flower. Flowering time is summer/early autumn. Stalk length is approximately 30 cm.

Aster novi-belgi (perennial aster, Michaelmas or Easter daisy)

There are several different varieties available, each producing sprays of fine-petalled daisies about the size of a 10 cent coin in white, mauve, lavender, pink, lavender-blue and purple. Good filler flower. Flowers appear in late summer. Stalk length is approximately 60 cm.

Aster lutea

Massed sprays of tiny star-like yellow open-petalled flowers. Much loved cut flower. Use as filler. Flowering time is spring/summer. Stalk length is approximately 60 cm.

Bouvardia longiflora

Terminal clusters of long tubular flowers with a jasmine-like scent and glossy green leaves. Use flowers individually for wedding work or whole flower head as filler flower. Flowering time is summer to autumn. Stalk length is approximately 30 cm (can be longer).

Bouvardia ternifolia

Terminal clusters of long, tubular red flowers up to 3 cm long. Use flowers individually for wedding work or whole flower head as filler flower. Flowering time is summer to autumn.

Stalk length is approximately 30 cm (can be longer).

Bouvardia leiantha
Terminal clusters of long, deep red flowers, 15 cm long. This species has been crossed with *B. longiflora* to produce varieties with flowers ranging in colour from white to salmon, pale and dark pink ('President Garfield') to orange-scarlet ('President Cleveland'). Use flowers individually for wedding work or whole flower head as filler flower. Flowering time is summer to autumn. Stalk length is approximately 30 cm (can be longer).

Bouvardia

Calendula 'Pacific Giant'
Large flat-faced orange or yellow blooms. Good for cutting. Secondary flower. Flowering time is winter/spring. Stalk length is 35 cm.

Centaurea cyanis (cornflower)
Flower heads are approximately the size of a 10 cent coin atop a straight stem. Flowers are pink, white and rich blue, the blue being the most renowned. Good secondary flower. Flowering time spring/summer. Stalk length is approximately 30 cm.

Chrysanthemum

Anemone chrysanthemum
Single daisy-like flower with green centre. Good secondary flower. Flowering time is autumn. Stalk length is over 50 cm.

Button chrysanthemum
Tiny pompom flowers are a little larger than a shirt button. Good filler flower. Flowering time is winter. Stalk length is over 50 cm.

Decorative chrysanthemum
Old-style round daisy. Good secondary flower. Flowering time is summer/autumn/winter. Stalk length is over 50 cm.

Pompom chrysanthemum
Pompom flowers. Good secondary flower. Flowering time is autumn. Stalk length is over 50 cm.

Semi-pom chrysanthemum
Similar appearance to the pompom chrysanthemum but the flowers are not as full. Good secondary flower. Flowering time is winter. Stalk length is over 50 cm.

Single chrysanthemum
Daisy flower. Good secondary flower. Flowering time is autumn/winter/summer. Stalk length is over 50 cm.

Spider chrysanthemum
Large cactus flower head. Most attractive. Good secondary or feature flower. Flowering time is autumn/winter. Stalk length is over 50 cm.

Quill chrysanthemum
Similar appearance to spider chrysanthemum but the petals twist into a quill. Good secondary flower. Flowering time is winter. Stalk length is over 50 cm.

Chrysanthemum frutescens (marguerite daisy)
Single-stemmed open-faced white, cream, pink, mauve or yellow daisies. Good secondary flower. Flowering time is summer. Stalk length is approximately 30 cm.

Chrysanthemum maximum (shasta daisy)
Large-flowered single or double open-faced daisies

with yellow centres. Good secondary flower. Flowering time is spring/summer. Stalk length is over 40 cm.

Dahlia

Cactus dahlia
Tall plants with large, shaggy, double, twisted petals. Available in mixed colours including orange, yellow, pink and red. Good secondary or feature flower. Flowering time is late summer to early autumn. Stalk length is approximately 30 cm.

Pompom dahlia
Small ball-shaped flower, available in mixed colours. Good secondary or filler flower. Flowering time is late summer to early autumn. Stalk length is approximately 30 cm.

Dahlia 'Red Skin'
Large semi-double red flowers and bronze foliage. Good secondary or feature flower. Flowering time is late summer to early autumn. Stalk length is approximately 30 cm.

Dahlia 'Diablo'
Large semi-double flower available in mixed shades of pink, orange, yellow and white. Good secondary or feature flower. Flowering time is late summer to early autumn. Stalk length is approximately 30 cm.

Delphinium (larkspur)
Tall spikes clustered with rich blue, lilac, pink or mauve flowers. Good outline flower. Flowering time is late spring/summer. Stalk length is over 40 cm.

Delphinium 'Magic Fountains'
Tall spikes of rich blue flowers. Good outline flower. Flowering time is late spring/summer. Stalk length is 90 cm.

Dianthus caryophyllus (carnation)

Field carnation
These carnations are grown outside in a field situation. They do not need disbudding. Available in 19 different colours. Good secondary flower. Flowering time all year. Stalk length is over 30 cm.

Micro carnation
Small single flower head atop a straight stem. The flowers are rose-coloured with garnet ring, light red, mauve-pink double, white, or purple double. Good secondary flower in small arrangements. Flowering time all year. Stalk length is over 20 cm.

Spray carnation
Smallish ruffled blooms. Available in 44 different colours. Centre of plant is disbudded, allowing side buds to flower. Good secondary flower. Flowering time all year. Stalk length is over 30 cm.

Standard/sim carnation
Large flower head on a single long stem. There are over 60 colours to choose from. Feature flower. Flowers are produced throughout the year. Stalk length is approximately 50 cm.

Dianthus chinensis
Similar appearance to a spray carnation. Limited colour range from vivid purple/lilac, lilac with white edge, dark burgundy, salmon pink with dark centre, dark violet/burgundy to a soft hot pink. Plants are grown under cover. Good secondary flower. Flowering time all year. Stalk length is over 30 cm.

Digitalis (foxglove)
Pretty flowering spikes with pendulous open bells. Colours range from cream to mauve, pink and purple with darker colouring in the flower centre. Good outline flower. Flowering time is spring. Stalk length is over 40 cm.

Erica (heath)
Usually flower heads are like beads dotted on the foliage. Flower colours include cream, pink, mauve and green. Great filler flower. Flowering time is autumn/spring. Stalk length 30 cm plus.

Eucomis comosa (pineapple lily)
Long, tubular formation made up of masses of creamy-white florets with dark centres, crowned with tiny, pineapple-type leaves. Feature flower. Flowering time is mid-summer. Stalk length is over 40 cm.

Eustoma russelliana (lisianthus)

The most popular colours at the moment are pink, blue and white as well as white edged with purple or rose pink. Available in single or double flower heads. Feature flower. Flowering time is spring/summer. Stalk length is over 30 cm.

Freesia

Flower colours include white, blue, rose pink, and yellow. Highly perfumed. Stem lengths range from miniature to giant. Good filler flower. Flowering time is spring. Stalk length is usually 30 cm plus.

Gardenia

Very fragrant waxy white flowers. Feature flower. Individual flowers can be wired for wedding work. Flowering time is usually summer.

Gerbera

There is a wide range of gerberas to choose from. Colours include white, cream, pink, red, bright yellow, orange, gold and apricot pink. Feature flower. Gerberas flower all year. Stalk length is over 40 cm.

Gladiolus (gladioli)

Wide range of flower colours. Stem length ranges from very short to long. Outline flower. Flowers are produced abundantly in spring/autumn; otherwise all year. Stalk length is usually over 60 cm.

Gypsophila paniculata 'Bristol fairy'

This plant produces fine sprays of the tiniest white flowers, like 'dots' on fine branching stems. Use as filler flower. Flowers are produced abundantly during spring/autumn; otherwise all year.

Heliconia

Unusual, waxy tropical blooms. Feature flowers. Flowering time for many varieties, including *Heliconia psittacorum*, is all year; other varieties flower intermittently. Stalk length is over 30 cm.

Hippeastrum

Large bell-shaped lilies. Usually red or red and white striped flowers; sometimes lime or pink tinted white. Feature flower. Flowering time is summer. Stalk length is approximately 40 cm.

Hydrangea

These large balls of open florets come in white, blue or pink. Blue is produced by acid soil, pink by lime soil. Feature or filler flower. Individual florets can be wired in wedding work. Flowering time is spring. Stalk length is 30 cm.

Iberis (candytuft)

Small white flower heads are clustered on straight stems. Good filler flower. Flowering time is summer. Stalk length is 30–40 cm.

Iris

Bearded iris

The flower head is similar to Dutch iris but is more ruffled and is available in a wider range of colours including many two-toned shades. Perfect feature flower. Flowering time is spring. Stalk length is over 40 cm.

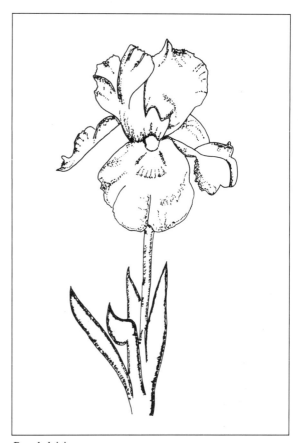

Bearded iris

Dutch iris

The most common Dutch iris flower is blue with a yellow tongue. Other flower colours include yellow with a white tongue, deep yellow and velvet blue. A perfect feature flower. Flowering time is spring. Stalk length is over 40 cm.

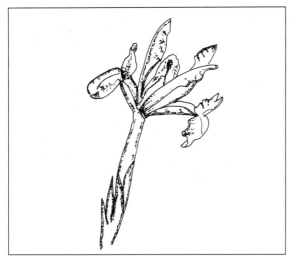

Dutch iris

English iris

Flowers are similar to Dutch iris but appear later in the season. Blue or white flowers. Lovely feature flower. Flowering time is late spring. Stalk length is over 40 cm.

Ixia (corn lily)

Lovely star-like tiny lily flowers in mixed colours. Good secondary or filler flower. Flowering time is spring. Stalk length is 30 cm.

Lathyrus odoratus (sweet pea)

Highly fragrant pea flowers in a variety of colours ranging from lilac and blue to rose pink and white. Filler flower. Flowering time is spring. Stalk length is approximately 20–30 cm.

Lavandula (lavender)

French, English and Spanish lavenders are used as cut flowers. French lavender is especially renowned for its perfume and abundant flowers. Will air-dry. Lovely filler flower. Flowering time is mainly winter/spring but sometimes continues into summer. Stalk length is approximately 20 cm.

Liatris spicata (gay feather)

Rose/purple or white spikes of long, slender feathery flower heads. An individualistic, modern-looking cut flower. Good outline or secondary flower. Flowering time is spring/summer. Stalk length is 60–90 cm.

Lilium (Asiatics)

Asiatic lilies are available in a wide variety of colours including pure white, creamy-white, light to dark pink, yellow, apricot, red, light orange and lime. Feature flower. Flowering time is summer. Stalk length is approximately 60 cm.

Lilium longiflorum (November or Christmas lily)

Showy, slender white trumpets. Feature flower. Flowering time is late spring/summer. Stalk length is approximately 60 cm.

Lilium (Oriental)

Similar to Asiatics but the petals are heavily spotted and curl right back when in full bloom. Popular colours are pinks, red and white. Feature flower. Flowering time is summer. Stalk length is approximately 60 cm.

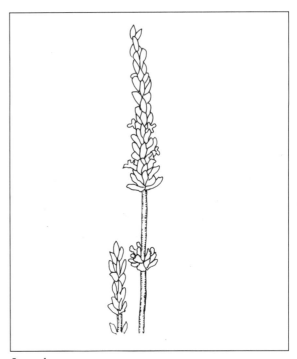

Lavender

Agapanthus orientalis

Alstroemeria

Anigozanthos (kangaroo paw)

Antirrhinium (snapdragon)

Anthurium andreanum (Anthurium lily)

Asparagus plumosa (asparagus fern)

Aster

Aster lutea

Banksia baxterii

Banksia coccinea (scarlet banksia)

Banksia prionotes

Banksia speciosa

Boronia heterophylla (red boronia)

Bowenia serrulata (Byfield fern)

Buxus (box)

Carnation (spray)

Carnation (standard or Sim)

Limonium (annual statice)

Tufts of papery flowers are borne on long branching stems. Flower colours include blue, violet, white, yellow, apricot and rose. Can be air-dried. Filler flower. Flowering time is spring/summer. Stalk length is approximately 60 cm.

Limonium hybrid 'Misty' range

Fine branching stems display tiny blue, pink or white flowers. A filler flower, often used in place of gypsophila. Very delicate. Flowering time is late winter/spring/summer. Stalk length is approximately 60 cm.

Limonium hybrid 'Oceanic' range

Similar to 'Misty' range but stems are stronger. Filler flower. Flowering time is late winter/spring/summer. Stalk length is approximately 60 cm.

Lunaria annua (honesty)

The seed heads form into attractive silvery discs once flowering is finished. The seed heads are used extensively as a dried flower. Filler flower. Flowering time is spring followed by discs.

Matricaria

Branching stems are topped with masses of small white daisy-like flowers with yellow centres. Very pretty filler flower. Flowering time is spring. Stalk length is approximately 60 cm.

Matthiola 'Giant Perfection' (stock)

Sweetly perfumed flower spikes in mixed colours including white, pink, lavender, red and purple. Good outline and filler flower. Flowering time is autumn/winter.

Moluccella laevis (bells of Ireland)

Green erect stems display clusters of green bell-like 'flowers' along their length. Good outline flower. Flowering time is spring. Stalk length 30–60 cm.

Narcissus 'Armada'

This bulb displays a daffodil flower with a broad rich golden perianth (outer petals) and large richly frilled cup of prominent deep tangerine-orange-red. Feature or secondary flower. Flowering time is spring. Stalk length is approximately 30 cm.

Narcissus 'Earlicheer'

This bulb produces a double creamy-white, heavily perfumed cluster of four to five daffodil flowers per stem. Secondary flower. Flowering time is spring. Stalk length is approximately 30 cm.

Narcissus 'Fortune'

This bulb produces a daffodil flower which is quite spectacular. It has a golden yellow perianth (outer petals) with a frilled orange cup. Feature or secondary flower. Flowering time is spring. Stalk length is approximately 30 cm.

Narcissus 'Glorification'

This bulb produces a magnificent daffodil flower showing a very smooth wide perianth (outer petals) and striking almost flat orange crown with exceptional frill. Good feature or secondary flower. Flowering time is spring. Stalk length is approximately 30 cm.

Narcissus 'King Alfred'

This bulb flower is perhaps the best known of the daffodils. It is a rich, pure yellow. Striking feature or secondary flower. Flowering time is spring. Stalk length is approximately 30 cm.

Narcissus 'Paperwhites'

These jonquil flowers are pure white and bear many flowers per stem. Secondary or filler flower. Flowering time is spring. Stalk length is at least 30 cm.

Narcissus 'Yellow Soleil D'or'

These jonquil flowers have a yellow perianth and an orange cup. Very pretty secondary or filler flower. Flowering time is spring. Stalk length at least 30 cm.

Nerine

White, pink or red bulb flowers. Interesting secondary flower. Flowering time is autumn/spring. Stalk length at least 30 cm.

Nymphea filifolia (water lily)

Common flower colours are white, pink, and mauve. Splendid feature flower or closed buds can be used to highlight an arrangement. Flowering time is spring. Stalk length is approximately 30 cm.

Ornithogalum

Open-petalled, white 20–30 mm flowers are borne in a tightly packed raceme which becomes quite cone-shaped as the flowers open. Varieties include 'Chincherinchee' and 'Star of Bethlehem'. Good secondary flower. Flowering time is late spring. Stalk length 20–30 cm.

Ornithogalum

Paeonia officinalis (paeony rose)

Varying shades of pink and white flowers with pink streaks. A lovely fragrant large flower. Good feature flower. Flowering time is spring/summer. Stalk length is approximately 30 cm.

Phlox paniculata (perennial phlox)

Tall stems massed with flat open florets. Flower colours include deep violet blue, soft pink, rich dark violet, salmon pink, pure white, bright red and blue. Filler flower. Flowering time is summer. Stalk length is approximately 30 cm.

Papaver (Iceland poppy)

Available in mixed colours including orange, yellow, white and red. Lovely secondary flower. Flowering time is winter/spring. Stalk length is approximately 30 cm.

Ranunculus

These corms produce ruffled flowers in mixed colours including red, yellow, white, orange and pink. A black ranunculus is also available. Good secondary or filler flower. Flowering time is spring. Stalk length to 30 cm.

Rosa (roses)

Roses are too numerous to mention all the varieties but here a few to get you started.

Rosa 'Bridal Pink' (floribunda)

A beautiful shell pink flower, popular for weddings as well as everyday arrangements. Feature flower. Flowering time is spring/summer/autumn. Stalk length is approximately 60 cm.

Rosa 'Gold Bunny' (floribunda)

A striking golden yellow rose. Feature flower. Flowering time is spring/summer/autumn. Stalk length is approximately 30 cm.

Rosa 'Mr Lincoln' (hybrid tea)

Deep red rose. Feature flower. Flowering time is spring/summer/autumn. Stalk length is approximately 60 cm.

Rosa 'Pascalli' (hybrid tea)

A lovely white rose, again popular for bridal work as well as general floristry. Feature flower. Flowering time is spring/summer/autumn. Stalk length is 30 cm.

Rosa 'Peter Frankenfield' (hybrid tea)

A cerise pink rose. Feature flower. Flowering time is spring/summer/autumn. Stalk length is approximately 60 cm.

Rosa 'Sonia' (floribunda)

A lovely apricot-pink rose. Feature flower. Flowering time is spring/summer/autumn. Stalk length is approximately 30 cm.

Scabiosa atropurpurea (sweet scabious, old maid's pincushion or mourning bride)

Flower colours range from pale to dark blue, purple, red, salmon pink, white, and rose. Both single and double flowers are available. Secondary flower. Flowering time is summer. Stalk length is 60–90 cm.

Scabiosa caucasica (pincushion flower or perennial scabiosa)

White to blue/mauve flowers. Secondary flower. Flowering time is summer. Stalk length is 50 cm.

Scabiosa (pincushion flower)

Stephanotis floribunda

Large, creamy-white jasmine shaped bells with a lovely perfume. Usually plucked from the stem and wired individually for wedding work. Feature or secondary flower. Flowering time is summer.

Trachelium (throatwort)

This plant features sprays of heads of tiny violet-blue or white flowers in clumps with slightly serrated, dark green, glossy leaves. A tall and slender flower producing a dramatic effect. Secondary or filler flower. Flowering time is summer. Stalk length 60 cm.

Polianthes tuberosa (tuberose)

Elongated clusters of perfumed white waxy flowers. Feature or outline flower. Flowering time is summer. Stalk length is at least 60 cm.

Tulipa (tulip)

Tulipa 'Apeldoorn'

A large brilliant scarlet flower. Feature flower. Flowering time is spring. Stalk length 30 cm plus.

Tulipa 'Beauty of Apeldoorn'

A large, golden yellow flower. Feature flower. Flowering time is spring. Stalk length 30 cm plus.

Tulipa 'High Noon'

A pink flower with a white reverse. Feature flower. Flowering time is spring. Stalk length 30 cm plus.

Tulipa 'Leen Vander Mark'

A red flower with a white edge. Feature flower. Flowering time is spring. Stalk length 30 cm plus.

Tulipa 'Monton'

Baby pink coloured flower. Feature flower. Flowering time is spring. Stalk length 30 cm plus.

Viola (violets)

Sweetly scented purple-faced tiny flowers. Filler flowers. Flowering time is spring. Stalk length is approximately 20 cm.

Watsonia

The pink or white flowers are reminiscent of gladioli but are finer in flower. Outline flower. Flowering time is spring/summer. Stalk length is 60–90 cm.

Watsonia

Zantedeschia (calla lily)
These trumpet-shaped flowers are available in an abundance of colours including salmon, black-red, red, orange, pink, yellow and pure white. Feature flower. Flowering time is winter/spring. Stalk length is 60 cm.

Zinnia 'Gold Medal Mix'
Truly superb double flowers approximately 10 cm across. Available in separate colours including cherry, orange, pink, purple, scarlet, white and yellow. Feature or secondary flower. Flowering time late summer to early autumn. Stalk length 30 cm.

Zinnia 'Happy Talk'
Twisted petals give these flowers a shaggy appearance, not unlike dahlias. Available in mixed colours including yellow, orange, purple and white. Feature or secondary flower. Flowering time is late summer to early autumn. Stalk length is approximately 30 cm.

Zinnia 'Showman'
Semi-double flowers are available in mixed colours including orange, red, yellow and cream. Secondary flowers. Flowering time is late summer to early autumn. Stalk length is approximately 30 cm.

East Coast and Inland Australian Natives

Acacia macradenia (zigzag wattle)
Zigzag branches are covered in a profusion of golden balls. Excellent vase life and graceful habit. Great filler flower. Flowers appear in spring with a stalk length of 60 cm plus.

Acacia perangusta (weeping Brisbane wattle)
Graceful weeping branches with fine leaves are highlighted by yellow flower balls in late winter/early spring. Filler flower. Stalk length is 60 cm plus.

Acacia podalyriifolia (Queensland silver wattle)
A small tree with round grey-green leaves, producing masses of golden flower balls in winter. Excellent filler flower. Stalk length is 60 cm plus.

Acacia spectabilis (glory wattle)
Pretty fern-like blue-green leaves are adorned with golden flower balls in winter. Good filler flower. Stalk length 60 cm plus.

Anigozanthos (kangaroo paw)

Anigozanthos 'Big Red'
Large, deep red kangaroo paw bearing spikes up to 1.5 m–2 m tall. Filler flower or useful for making arrangement outlines. Flowers appear in spring/summer.

Anigozanthos 'Dwarf Delight'
Unusual coloured apricot-pink paws. The stems are covered in fine red hairs. Good filler flower. Flowers appear in spring/summer. Stalk length is 40–50 cm.

Anigozanthos 'Early Spring'
Bright red flower spikes. Good filler flower. Flowers appear at the end of winter through to summer. Stalk length is 40–50 cm.

Anigozanthos 'Emerald Glow'
Spectacular emerald/turquoise flowers which contrast with the pink glowing stems. The foliage, unlike other kangaroo paws, is fine, almost onion-like in appearance. Good filler flower. Flowering time is late winter to summer. Stalk length up to 50 cm.

Anigozanthos 'Fire Opal'
Showy orange/red spikes with green throats. Good filler flower and, like other kangaroo paws, is good outline material for arrangements. Flowering time is winter. Stalk length is 50 cm.

Anigozanthos 'Southern Aurora Yellow Rock'
Pure yellow spikes. Good filler flower. Flowering time is late winter/spring. Stalk length is 40–50 cm.

Anigozanthos 'Southern Aurora Surouge'
Deep red spikes. Good filler flower. Flowering

time is late winter/spring. Stalk length is 40–50 cm.

Anigozanthos 'Southern Aurora Pink Fuzz'
Light pink spikes. Good filler flower. Flowering time is late winter/spring. Stalk length is 40–50 cm.

Anigozanthos 'Southern Aurora Strawberry Whirl'
Medium pink-coloured spikes. Good filler flower. Flowering time is late winter/spring. Stalk length is 40–50 cm.

Anigozanthos 'Southern Aurora Suffuse'
Dark pink spikes. Good filler flower. Flowering time is late winter/spring. Stalk length is 40–50 cm.

Anigozanthos 'Southern Aurora Solace'
Apricot/yellow spikes. Good filler flower. Flowering time is late winter/spring. Stalk length is 40–50 cm.

Anigozanthos 'Southern Aurora Orange Crush'
Bright orange-coloured spikes. Good filler flower. Flowering time is late winter/spring. Stalk length is 40–50 cm.

Baeckea 'La Petite'
Dainty bright green foliage with massed tiny white flowers and arching branches. Excellent filler flower. Flowering time is summer to winter. Stalk length is 30–40 cm

Baeckea 'Mt Tozer'
Shiny, green, rounded, small leaves adorned with masses of white flowers. A truly magnificent filler flower. Flowering time is summer. Stalk length is approximately 60 cm.

Banksia ericifolia (heath leaf banksia)
Pine-like foliage bears medium-sized, bright orange banksia brushes. Feature or secondary flower. Flowering time is autumn to winter. Stalk length is approximately 30 cm (can be shorter).

Banksia ericifolia 'Burgundy Form'
Rich burgundy-coloured, medium-sized brushes. Feature or secondary flower. Flowering time is autumn and winter. Stalk length is approximately 30 cm (can be shorter).

Banksia 'Giant Candles' (B. collina × B. ericifolia)
Light green pine-like leaves and gigantic bright orange upright brushes (similar to *B. ericifolia* flowers but much larger). Use as feature flower. Flowering time is autumn. Stalk length is approximately 30 cm.

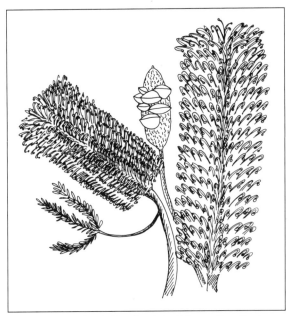

Banksia ericifolia (left); *Banksia* 'Giant Candles' (right)

Banksia robur (swamp banksia)

Banksia robur (swamp banksia)

A truly beautiful banksia featuring broad, dark green leaves. The banksia brush glows a striking dark blue/green colour. Use as a feature flower. Flowering time is spring and summer. Stalk length is over 30 cm.

Banksia spinulosa var. collina (hill banksia)

Golden banksia brushes are backed by fine green, serrated leaves. A good feature flower. Flowering time is autumn. Stalk length varies up to 30 cm.

Bauera rubioides (pink dog rose)

Pink or white open-petalled flowers and hairy green leaves. Good filler flower. Flowering times are spring/summer. Stalk length is approximately 60 cm.

Bauera sessiliflora (showy dog rose)

Pretty, soft, green, thick foliage which becomes massed with mauve flowers, displaying a definite black eye. Filler flower. Flowers appear in spring/summer. Stalk length is approximately 60 cm.

Blandfordia grandiflora (Christmas bells)

Flowering spikes are clustered with red and yellow bells. Use as secondary flower. Flowering time is spring/summer and autumn. Stalk length is approximately 50 cm.

Boronia serrulata (native rose)

Masses of pretty pink, fragrant bells. Excellent filler flower. Flowering time is spring. Stalk length is approximately 30 cm.

Ceratopetalum gummiferum (NSW Christmas bush)

In season, flowers are prolific, starting out white in spring followed by red calyxes in summer. Wonderful filler flower. Stalk length is approximately 60 cm.

Ceratopetalum gummiferum (Christmas bush)

Blandfordia grandiflora (Christmas bells)

Clianthus formosa (Sturt's desert pea)

Clianthus formosa (Sturt's desert pea)

Long clusters of scarlet pea flowers, each with a prominent black dome in the centre. Feature flower. Flowering time is spring/summer. Stalk length is approximately 30 cm.

Crinum pedunculatum (river lily)
Spikes of large white lily-like flowers with bright green leaves up to 1 m long. Feature flower. Flowering time is summer. Stalk length is approximately 30 cm.

Curcuma australasica (Cape York lily)
Lily-like plant which produces spectacular pink or yellow flower heads approximately 10 cm in diameter. Feature flower. Flowering time is late spring. Stalk length is 30 cm.

Curcuma australasica (Cape York lily)

Dodonaea pinnata (hop bush)
Inconspicuous flowers are followed by wonderful red seed capsules which make an unusual filler flower. The seed capsules are produced in summer. Stalk length is approximately 60 cm.

Dodonaea triquetra (hop bush)
Inconspicuous flowers are followed by unusual green seed capsules. Makes a great filler. Seed capsules appear in summer. Stalk length is approximately 60 cm.

Epacris impressa (common heath)
This plant is the floral emblem of Victoria and grows to 1 metre in height, displaying delicate pink/red bells amidst fine, spiky leaves. Filler flower. Flowering time is spring. Stalk length is approximately 30 cm.

Eriostemon australasius (wax flower)
Stems are massed with large, rich pink, star-like wax flowers opening from pink buds. Wonderful filler flower. Flowering time is spring. Stalk length is approximately 30 cm.

Eriostemon myoporoides (wax flower)
Bright green foliage massed with pink buds, opening to small star-like wax flowers. Great filler flower. Flowering time is spring. Stalk length is approximately 30 cm.

Eucalyptus pachyphylla
Clusters of red-capped, yellow gum blossoms. Filler or secondary flower; also can be used as a feature in wedding bouquets. Flowering time is late winter/spring. Stalk length is 30 cm.

Eucalyptus ptychocarpa (swamp bloodwood)
Large dark green leaves and masses of 7 cm pink to red blossoms followed by attractive gum nuts. Use as a filler, secondary flower or feature flower. Stalk length is 30 cm.

Eucalyptus ptychocarpa (swamp bloodwood)

Eucalyptus yalatensis
The red or lemon-coloured buds are excellent as fillers. Harvest in mid-winter. Stalk length is 30 cm.

Grevillea 'Coochin Hills'

Small creamy yellow flowers. Good secondary flower in bowl or wired work. Flowers most of the year but peaks in spring. Stalk length 30 cm plus.

Grevillea 'Honey Gem'

Rich golden yellow brushes. Wonderful secondary or feature flower in bowl or wired work. Flowers most of the year but peaks in spring. Stalk length 30 cm plus.

Grevillea 'Kay Williams'

Pink brushes with cream styles. Secondary or feature flower in bowl or wired work. Flowers most of the year but peaks in spring. Stalk length is 30 cm plus.

Grevillea 'Majestic'

Rich crimson/pink brushes with cream styles. Good secondary or feature flower in bowl or wired work. Flowers all year but peaks in spring. Stalk length 30 cm plus.

Grevillea 'Misty Pink'

Unusual pale pink-coloured brush with cream styles. Very pretty secondary or feature flowers in bowl or wired work. Flowers all year but peaks in spring. Stalk length 30 cm plus.

Grevillea 'Moonlight'

Displays creamy yellow (sometimes called white) body and styles. Pretty secondary or feature flower in bowl or wired work. Flowers all year but peaks in spring. Stalk length 30 cm plus.

Grevillea 'Pink Parfait'

Deep watermelon-pink flowers. Excellent secondary or feature flower for bowl or wired work. Flowers all year but peaks in spring. Stalk length 30 cm plus.

Grevillea 'Pink Surprise'

Rich pink brush with cream styles. Wonderful secondary or feature flower in bowl or wired work. Flowers all year but peaks in spring. Stalk length 30 cm plus.

Grevillea 'Poorinda Blondie'

Masses of apricot toothbrush flowers in spring/summer. Good filler flower or for use in outlining an arrangement. Stalk length is approximately 60 cm.

Grevillea 'Poorinda Elegance'

Beautiful glossy green foliage and masses of two-toned yellow and red spider flowers. Excellent filler flower. Flowering time is spring to autumn. Stalk length is approximately 60 cm.

Grevillea 'Sylvia'

Rich watermelon-coloured body with cerise styles. Wonderful secondary or feature flower in either bowl or wired work. Flowers all year but peaks in spring. Stalk length is 30 cm plus.

Helichrysum bracteatum 'Dargan Hill Monarch' (everlasting daisy or strawflower)

The flowers are produced throughout the year and are open petalled, measuring 8 cm diameter. Colours range from pure white to pale lemon and bright yellow. Other hybrids to look out for are 'Lemon Monarch', 'White Monarch', 'Cockatoo' and 'Princess of Wales'. Flowers are long lasting when fresh, and everlasting when dried. (Must be picked in bud otherwise petals turn backwards as they dry). Stalk length is approximately 30 cm.

Helichrysum 'Bright Bikini' (everlasting daisy)

These come in a wide variety of colours ranging from deep red to pink, cream and yellow. The flowers are about the size of a 10 cent coin when fully opened. Pick when first or second row of petals have turned down for best results. Use fresh or dried as a secondary flower. Flowering time is spring. Stalk length is approximately 30 cm.

Helipterum (everlasting daisy or paper daisy)

Pink or white, flat, open flower usually with a distinctive black ring around the centre of the petals. Use fresh or dried as a secondary flower. Flowering time is spring. Stalk length is approximately 30 cm.

Ixodia achillioides (South Australian or mountain daisy)

This plant displays clusters of tiny white flowers which are easy to dye. Use as a fresh or dried filler flower. Flowering time is summer. Stalk length is approximately 40–60 cm.

Carnation (micro)

Chrysanthemum

Chrysanthemum

Chamaelaucium uncinatum
(Geraldton wax)

Cymbidium Winter Wonder

Bc Mount Hood (*Cattleya* alliance)

Lc Irene Finney 'York' (*Cattleya* alliance)

Cymbidium Clarisse Austin 'Bimerah'

Cymbidium Terama

Cymbidium Winter Wonder 'Jeannie'

Cymbidium Wamara × Kerta

Cymbidium Sensation × Betley Radiance

Cymbidium Zuma Boyd × Arcadian Melody

Dendrobium Bardo Rose

Dendrobium canaliculatum

Dendrobium delicatum

Dendrobium falcorostrum

Dendrobium gracillimum

Dendrobium kingianum

Dendrobium Lady Gem Profusion

Dendrobium bigibbum 'Superbum' 'Col' HCC-AOC

29

Dryandra formosa (showy dryandra)

Delphinium

Dendrobium (Singapore Orchid)

Daviesia cordata (Bookleaf) dried foliage

Erica sessiliflora (green erica or heath)

Eucalypt kruseana (Kruse's mallee)

Eustoma russelliana (lisianthus)

Freesia

Leptospermum flavescens 'Cardwell'
Light green weeping branches are covered in white tea-tree flowers and pink buds. Great filler flower. Flowering time is late winter/spring. Stalk length is 50 cm plus. A pink form 'Pink Cascade' is now available.

Melaleuca thymifolia (pink lace)
Small, oval, blue-green leaves and lacy, pale pink flowers which cling to the stem. Good filler flower. Flowers are produced throughout the year. Stem length is approximately 60 cm.

Olearia tomentosa 'Compact' (native daisy)
A very pretty flower when in season. The conifer-like foliage acts as a foil to the masses of yellow-centred daisy-like flowers. Flowering time is spring. Stalk length is approximately 30 cm.

Oreocallis wickhamii (North Queensland tree waratah)
Brilliant orange/red clustered flower spikes. Feature flower. Flowering time is spring/summer. Stalk length is approximately 60 cm.

Patersonia sericea (native iris)
Mauve flower resembles a small iris; perfect for oriental arrangements. Pretty secondary flower or feature flower. Flowering time is late winter/spring/summer. Stalk length is 30 cm.

Pimelea linifolia 'Pink Form'
This plant has fine foliage and produces masses of pink button flowers throughout the year. Filler flower. Stalk length is approximately 30 cm.

Stirlingia
Masses of fluffy, small grey 'balls' are borne along the stems. Can be dried and colour dyed. Also used in bud form. Outline material or filler flower. Flowering time is summer. Stalk length if 60 cm.

Telopea speciosissima (waratah)
The waratah is a well known and popular cut flower valued for its large, rich red flowers. Other varieties for different areas are *T. oreades* (Gippsland waratah) and *T. truncata* (Tasmanian waratah). Feature flower. Flowering time is spring. Stalk length is approximately 60 cm.

Oreocallis wickhamii (North Queensland tree waratah)

Telopea speciosissima (waratah)

Telopea 'Shady Lady' (hybrid waratah)
The flower is as stunning as the original waratah but is easier to grow in most areas. A prolific flowerer. Use as feature flower. Flowering time is spring. Stalk length is approximately 60 cm.

Thryptomene calycina

A popular cut flower with fine foliage and masses of tiny, pink, open flowers and pink buds. Renowned as a filler flower. Can be dried using glycerine. Flowering time is winter. Stalk length is approximately 60 cm.

Thryptomene saxicola

Graceful slender branches are frosted with white/pink flowers. Use as filler flower. Flowering time is winter. Stalk length is approximately 60 cm.

Xylomelum pyriforme (woody pear)

This plant is grown for its pear-shaped nuts. Nuts are everlasting but should be stored carefully as they can become mildewed. Flowers appear during spring, followed by nuts. Stalk length up to 60 cm.

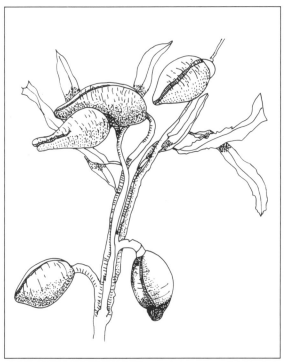

Xyolemelum pyriforme (woody pear)

West Coast Australian Natives

Acacia rossei (wattle)

Upright branches covered in rich yellow clusters of fluffy ball flowers. After flowering, this wattle bears unusual seed pods. Flowers appear winter/spring. It is a lovely but short-lived filler flower. Branches up to 1.5 m in length.

Actinodium cunninghamii (Albany daisy)

Flowers are daisy-like in appearance with white petals and pinky-red centres, measuring up to 4 cm diameter. Flowers winter/spring with a stalk length up to 60 cm.

Actinodium cunninghamii (Albany daisy)

Agonis linearifolia

Spikes of white, rice-type flowers are massed along the stems. Flowers can be used fresh or air dried. Flowers appear in spring/summer and branches can be up to 1.5 m in length.

Anigozanthos (kangaroo paw)

Anigozanthos bicolor
Flowers are red, green and yellow in colour. Flowering time is spring/summer. Stalk length is approximately 60 cm.

Anigozanthos manglesii
Striking red and green paws appear in spring/summer. Stalk length is up to 1.5 m.

Anigozanthos viridis
All green flower. Flowering time is spring. Stalk length is 1 m.

Astartea ambigua
Pale pink flowers, 1 cm in diameter, occur in clusters within the leaf axils. Flowers appear in winter/spring. Branches up to 60 cm in length.

Banksia ashbyi
Bright orange, squat brushes are formed in late winter to summer. Stalk length is up to 60 cm.

Banksia baxteri (bird's nest banksia)
Creamy/yellow brushes are ideal for colour dyeing. The brushes are squat balls and appear summer/autumn. Slender stalks up to 60 cm.

Banksia burdettii (Burdett's banksia)
Bright orange brushes appear in spring/summer. Stalk length is around 60 cm.

Banksia coccinea (scarlet banksia)
This is a most attractive and sought-after cut flower. The flowers are squat, red and grey striped brushes surrounded by wide, rounded, dark green leaves. The plant benefits from pruning. Flowering time is winter to early spring. Stalks grow to approximately 60 cm.

Banksia hookeriana (Hooker's banksia)
Popular cream-coloured medium-sized banksia flower. Flowering time is winter/spring. The long slender stalks grow to 60 cm.

Banksia media (golden flowering banksia)
This plant features rich yellow banksia flowers and attractive foliage. Flowering time is spring. Stalk length to 60 cm.

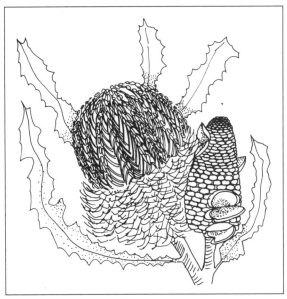

Banksia menziessi (Menzies' banksia)

Banksia menziesii (Menzies' banksia)
Rich pink/mauve and yellow brushes. Stalk length at least 60 cm.

Banksia prionotes (acorn banksia)
Large cream-coloured heads which dye and dry well. Marvellous feature flower for large arrangements. Flowering time is autumn/spring. Stalk length is 60 cm and over.

Banksia speciosa (showy banksia)
Large, showy yellow-green brushes. Spectacular feature flowers for use in large arrangements. Flowering time is summer/autumn. Stalk length is at least 60 cm.

Beaufortia sparsa
Stiff green branches bear small, brilliant orange/red bottlebrush flowers which are popular in fresh and dried arrangements. Flowering time is summer/autumn. Stalk length is approximately 60 cm.

Boronia heterophylla (red boronia)
Although this plant is referred to as 'red' the bell flowers are more of a hot pink colour and abundantly adorn the finely-leafed branches. Flowering time is late autumn to spring. Stalk length is approximately 60 cm.

Boronia megastigma (brown boronia)
Highly fragrant, brown and yellow bell-like flowers. A wonderful filler. Flowering time is winter. Stalk length is approximately 60 cm.

Chamelaucium axillare (Esperance wax)
An unusual wax flower because its fine, small flowers start off white before turning red, producing simultaneous red and white flowers on one small shrub. Excellent filler flower. Flowering time is winter to late spring. Stalk length is approximately 30 cm.

Chamelaucium uncinatum 'Alba' (Geraldton wax)
Dainty five-petalled white wax flowers with green centres. Wonderful filler flower for weddings and baby baskets. Flowering time is winter/spring. Stalk length is 60 cm plus.

Chamelaucium uncinatum 'Purple Pride' (Geraldton wax)
A rich purple form of *C. uncinatum*. Wonderful general filler flower. Flowering time is winter/spring. Stalk length is 60 cm plus.

Chamelaucium uncinatum 'Wilson's Selection' (Geraldton wax)
Delicate five-petalled wax flowers. Again, a wonderful filler flower. Flowering time is winter to late spring. Stalk length is 60 cm plus.

Conospermum stoechadis (smoke bush)
This small erect shrub produces flowers which are blue/grey, shaggy, woolly wisps. A good fresh or dried filler flower. Flowering time is spring/summer. Stalk length is around 60 cm.

Craspedia uniflora (billy buttons)
This unusual member of the daisy family has leaves low to the ground out of which flowers or 'buttons' appear on long spikes. The flower heads are quite substantial—approximately the diameter of a 10 cent coin. Use fresh or dried for accent. Flowering time is spring/summer. Stalk length is up to 45 cm.

Darwinia leiostyla (mountain bell)
Attractive red and white bells. Dainty foliage and a good filler flower. See also white *D. meeboidii* (Cranebrook bell), *D. nieldiana* (fringe bell) and

D. citriodora. Flowering time is spring/summer. Stalk length is 60 cm.

Dryandra formosa (showy dryandra)
This is a cut flower renowned worldwide for its finely serrated, rich green leaves and golden-rust rosette flowers or 'brushes'. The flower heads are approximately 6 cm in diameter and the stems are long and fine, perfect for use in all floral work. Good as a fresh or dried flower in small arrangements or as secondary or filler flower in others. Flowering time is spring to early summer. Stalk length is approximately 60 cm.

Dryandra praemorsa (cut-leaved dryandra)
This shrub produces yellow/green brushes similar in size to *D. formosa* although the flowers have a slightly heavier appearance. Good as feature or secondary flower for baskets, bowls or driftwood. Flowering time is spring. Stalk length is over 30 cm.

Eucalyptus burracoppinensis
Both the lime/yellow buds and cream flowers are used as a filler, especially for those weddings with a difference. Harvesting time is autumn/winter; stalk length 30 cm plus.

Eucalyptus caesia (gungurru)
Although classed as a small tree, this eucalypt grows to 7.5 m if allowed. It bears heavy clusters of dusty pink to red flowers on powdery grey branches. The gum nuts are also an attractive powdery grey colour. Use fresh gum blossoms for bowl or baskets as well as for wedding bouquets; use gum nuts fresh or dried. Harvest in winter/spring. Stalk length is over 60 cm.

Eucalyptus clelandi
Silver and apricot buds appear during winter/spring. Lovely filler. Stalk length is 30 cm plus.

Eucalyptus erythrocorys (illyarrie)
Brilliant red flowers with bright gold stamens. Has been grown successfully on the East Coast in low humidity, dry areas. Gum nuts are well sized, fluted and attractive. It can be pruned successfully. Harvest in summer/autumn. Stalk length is approximately 60 cm.

Eucalyptus ficifolia (red flowering gum)

Usually produces brilliant scarlet flowers although orange and pink have been recorded. Good sized gum nuts. Harvest in late summer. Stalk length is 30 cm plus. Has been grown successfully on the East Coast.

Eucalyptus ficifolia (red flowering gum)

Eucalyptus erythrocorys (illyarrie)

Eucalyptus macrocarpa (mottlecah)

This shrub grows to approximately 3 m in height and bears attractive silvery/grey foliage and striking crimson flowers. A notable feature of this plant is its large (5–7 cm diameter) gum nuts which are disc-like and most distinctive. Harvest mainly during winter/spring, although blossoming can be irregular. Use flowers, foliage and gum nuts. Stalk length is up to 60 cm.

Eucalyptus macrocarpa (mottlecah)

Eucalyptus orbifolia

Purple buds are formed during winter. Striking filler. Stalk length is up to 60 cm.

Eucalyptus plenissima

A blaze of pink/orange buds appear during spring/summer. Especially lovely for wedding work. Up to 60 cm stalk length.

Eucalyptus pterocarpa (orange fluted gum)

Grow this one for the buds which are absolutely stunning. They are orange/apricot in colour, and as the name indicates, fluted in appearance. Has been successfully grown on the East Coast in dry non-humid areas. Harvest in late autumn to summer. Stalk length is up to 60 cm.

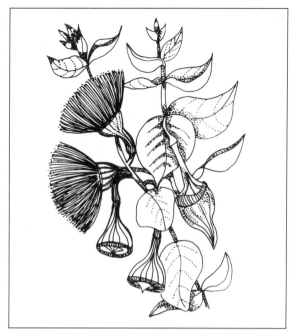

Eucalyptus rhodantha (rose mallee)

Eucalyptus rhodantha (rose mallee)
This tree grows to 3 m in height and displays attractive silvery/grey heart-shaped leaves, offsetting the crimson flowers which sometimes measure 6 cm across. The gum nuts are cap or cone-shaped and extremely attractive. Harvest irregularly throughout the year. Stalk length is up to 60 cm.

Eucalyptus tetragona (tallerack)
This eucalypt has lovely silver-blue foliage and white, square-shaped stems and grey/white gum nuts along the stems. The flowers are white. Used mainly for foliage and gum nuts. Harvest during summer. Stalk length is up to 1 m.

Eucalyptus tetraptera (square-fruited mallee)
Square-shaped, pendulous red buds are followed by pink flowers during autumn/winter. Stalk length is up to 60 cm.

Eucalyptus youngiana (large-fruited mallee)
Brown/bronze buds and yellow, pink or red flowers. The flowers open to approximately 8 cm in diameter. A dramatic addition to any arrangement. Harvest during winter/spring. Stalk length is 60 cm. Also native to South Australia.

Geleznowia verrucosa (bell flower)
This is a small shrub with an almost succulent appearance. The flower looks like a miniature, open, waxy rose and is excellent as a filler. Flowering time is spring. Stalk length is 30–40 cm.

Geleznowia verrucosa (bell flower)

Grevillea candelabroides
This shrub needs full sun to produce its profusion of long, white, candle-shaped flowers. Prune after flowering for best results. Flowering time is summer. Stalk length is 30–40 cm.

Grevillea wickhamii
Lovely hanging bunches of red/orange spider flowers are a feature of this plant, which grows to 3 m in height. Good filler. Flowering time is winter/spring. Stalk length up to 60 cm.

Hakea bucculenta
This popular hakea is one of the grass-leafed varieties, displaying long, rich green-coloured foliage and brilliant scarlet flower spikes (not unlike grevillea flowers). Flowering time is winter. Stalk length is up to 60 cm.

Hakea laurina (pincushion hakea)

A truly magnificent flower. This small tree has eucalypt-like leaves which are bronze when young. The leaves offset the flowers which are red cushions with pink stamens. Also of interest are the seed pods or 'hakea nuts', sometimes known as 'leopard nuts'. Flowers appear in late autumn to early winter. Stalk length varies; long branches.

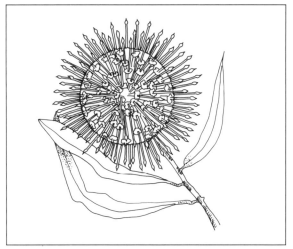

Hakea laurina (pincushion daisy)

Helipterum (everlasting daisy)

Hakea laurina—leopard nuts

Helipterum roseum (everlasting daisy)

These flowers are daisy-like in appearance with a flat open face, up to 5 cm in diameter, exposing a dark, gold rimmed centre. Can be used fresh or dried as filler or feature flower in small basket arrangements. Dried flowers are also good for decorating hats, wall brooms, etc. Flowering time is spring/summer. Stalk length is up to 60 cm.

Hypocalymma robustum (Swan River myrtle)

The abundant tiny flowers are produced along the branches and are five petalled and pinky mauve in colour. A very dainty filler flower which transports well. Flowering time is late winter/spring; stalk length up to 60 cm.

Isopogon dubius (drumsticks)

This bushy shrub is the smallest of this genus, growing to 1 m × 1 m. The attractive 'drumstick' flower heads have a feathered or fringed appearance. Use as a filler flower. Flowering time is spring. Stalk length is approximately 60 cm.

Kunzea pulchella

This plant features a spectacular display of brilliant red bottlebrush-type flowers contrasted by silvery foliage. Flowering time is spring/autumn. Stalk length is 30–60 cm.

Lachnostachys eriobotrya (lamb's tails)

Grey woolly foliage and white cottonwool-type clumps of flowers. An unusual filler flower. Flowering time is spring. Stalk length is approximately 60 cm.

Lechenaultia biloba (blue lechenaultia)

Brilliant blue flowers. Prune hard after flowering to get the best results. Also try *L. formosa* (red lechenaultia). Good as filler flower or secondary flower for small arrangements. Flowers appear in spring. Stalk length is approximately 60 cm.

Loudonia aurea

The brilliant yellow flowers are produced on long, slender stems. Common around low rainfall areas of Western and South Australia. A bright and attractive filler flower or feature flower for oriental-style work. Flowers appear in spring/ summer with a stalk length of approximately 60 cm plus.

Melaleuca huegelli

This plant displays a contrast of colour between the pinky/purple buds and white flowers. Flower heads grow to approximately 10 cm long and can be dried successfully. Also try *M. nematophylla* for 4 cm pink pompom everlasting flowers. Use as feature flower or filler. Flowering time is spring/summer. Stalk length is over 60 cm.

Melaleuca suberosa

Flowers are fluffy pink heads which dry readily if hung upside down. Use as a fresh or dried filler flower. Flowers appear in spring with a stalk length up to 60 cm.

Petrophile linearis (narrow-leaf cone bush)

This genus is closely related to *Isopogon*. The attractive flowers are pink and shaggy headed. After flowering the spikes form pine-like cones. Excellent as an interesting feature or secondary flower. Flowering time is spring/summer. Stalk length is approximately 40 cm.

Pityrodia axillaris (woolly foxglove)

This plant features beautiful pink bell flowers against soft grey foliage. Filler flower. Flowering time is spring. Stalk length is approximately 70 cm.

Ptilotus exaltatus (mulla mulla)

This plant produces white and pink furry flowers. Good filler flower. There are about 100 species of *Ptilotus* throughout Australia. Flowering time is spring/summer. Stalk length is approximately 60 cm.

Pultenaea dasyphuylla

The pea-shaped flowers are brilliant red, yellow, orange or purple and are produced in clumps at the end of the stems, surrounded by feathery silver and green leaves. Filler flower or feature flower on driftwood. Flowering time is spring. Stalk length is up to 60 cm.

Regelia velutina

Brilliant red bottlebush-type flowers covered with gold anthers, on spindly green stems. Use as a filler flower or secondary flower where bright colour and a rustic atmosphere is required. Flowers appear in spring/summer. Stalk length is up to 60 cm.

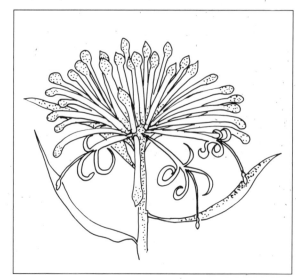

Petrophile linearis (narrow-leaf cone bush)

Grevillea 'Moonlight'

Grevillea 'Sylvia'

Gypsophila 'Bristol Fairy'

Heliconia

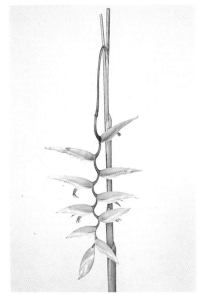

Heliconia charteacea
'Sexy Pink Hanger'

Iris

Helichrysum

Lachnostachys verbascifolia (lamb's tail)

39

Leucadendron coniferum
(Christmas cone)

Leucadendron 'Silvan Red'

Leucadendron stelligerum (male)

Leucospermum cordifolium
(pincushion protea)

Liatris (gay feather)

Lilium (Oriental lily)

Lilium (Asiatic lily)

Lilium longiflorum (Christmas lily)

Ricinocarpus tuberculatus (wedding bush)

A wonderful shrub to grow which will provide flowers during the heat of summer. Produces massed displays of waxy-white flowers over arching branches. The foliage is dark green. Prune after flowering. Use in branch form for large displays or wire clusters for wedding work. Flowering time is summer. Stalk length is 60 cm plus.

Thysanotus multiflorus (fringed lily)

A clumping plant with strap-like foliage and fringed iris-type mauve flowers. Good for oriental style and water scene arrangements or wherever European iris is used. Flowering time is spring. Stalk length is 30 cm.

Waitzia acuminata

Thysanotus multiflorus (fringed lily)

Verticordia plumosa

This plant produces masses of tiny, woolly purple-pink flowers which totally obscure the leaves. Can be grown on the East Coast of Australia. The flowers are easily air-dried but its use as a dried flower is perhaps not as popular as other members of this genus, e.g. *V. browneii* (cauliflower morrison) or *V. nitens* (golden nitens). All species are used as fresh or dried filler flowers. Flowering time is summer. Stalk length is approximately 60 cm.

Waitzia acuminata

This plant is classed as an everlasting daisy. The dainty globe-type heads appear singularly or in groups on slender stems and have a papery outline of petals. They come in a wide colour range, varying from white to pink to rich yellow/orange. They do well in most states, except Queensland and Tasmania. Use fresh or dried as a filler flower. Flowering time is spring and summer. Stalk length is approximately 45 cm.

Xylomelum angustifolium (woody pear)

A tree valued in the cut flower industry for its pear-shaped nuts. It is not widely cultivated. Nuts are everlasting but should be stored carefully as they can become mildewed. Flowers appear during summer, followed by nuts. Stalk length up to 60 cm.

Note: Many West Coast Australian natives can be grown on the East Coast or inland where climate is non-humid and soil is sandy or at least well drained.

Tasmanian Natives

Acacia dealbata (silver wattle)
A feathery-leaved wattle producing masses of yellow flower balls which make a truly spectacular display. Sold as a cut flower overseas. Good filler flower. Flowering time is late winter. Stalk length is approximately 60 cm.

Banksia marginata (honeysuckle banksia)
The brushes are cream to greeny/yellow-coloured and well formed. Use as feature flower. Stems are approximately 30 cm.

Blandfordia punicea (Christmas bells)
The straight stem displays clusters of bell-shaped flowers. The flowers are deep red on the outside and yellow inside. Very dramatic secondary or filler flower. Flowering time is spring/summer. Stalk length is approximately 30 cm.

Boronia pilosa (pink boronia)
Pink open-petalled flowers are formed in clusters at the end of the stems. Pretty filler flower. Flowering time is spring/summer. Stalk length is 30 cm.

Cassinia aculeata (dolly bush)
The leaves are narrow and tightly rolled. When in flower, branches terminate in a cluster of shorter branches, each bearing a mass of pink buds and tiny, white, rice-like flower heads. A pretty filler flower. Flowering time is summer. Stalk length is approximately 60 cm.

Dillwynia floribunda (parrot pea)
Masses of brick red to orange/yellow pea flowers are produced on slender branches. Filler flower. Flowering time is spring/summer. Stalk length is 30 cm plus.

Epacris impressa (heath)
This plant displays bell-like flowers in white, pink or red. Filler flower. Flowering time is autumn to summer. Stalk length is 30 cm.

Eriostemon verrucosus (wax flower)
White or pink starry wax flowers are borne along the length of the stem. A delicate and pretty filler flower. Flowering time is spring. Stalk length is 30 cm.

Helichrysum scorpioides (scorpion everlasting daisy; strawflower)
Bright yellow daisies for use fresh or dried. Small secondary flower. Flowering time is spring/summer. Stalk length is 30 cm.

Olearia stellulata (Tasmanian daisy bush)
Numerous white daisy-like flowers are borne at the end of slender branches. Filler flower. Flowering time is spring/summer. Stalk length is 30 cm.

Pimelea nivea (cotton bush)
White, cream or pink flowers are borne in dense heads at the end of the branches. Lovely filler flower. Flowering time is spring/summer. Stalk length is approximately 60 cm.

Telopea truncata (Tasmanian waratah)
Scarlet, deep red or rarely clear yellow waratah flowers. Styles are looser than NSW species (*T. speciosissima*) although it is still a stunning feature flower. Flowering time is summer. Stalk length is 60 cm.

Tetratheca pilosa (lilac bells)
Deep purple or white bells are clustered at the top of the narrow-leaved stems. Each flower features four black anthers hanging down from within. Use as filler flower. Flowering time is spring/summer. Stalk length is approximately 30 cm.

South African Plants

Leucadendron comicum
Female plants are used for their cones rather than flowers. Harvest in spring/summer. Stalk length is approximately 30 cm plus.

Leucadendron comiferum
Female plants are used for their cones in late spring. Stalk length is 30 cm plus.

Leucadendron daphnoides
Female plants display a most attractive flower, being yellow in winter then turning pink in spring followed by cones. Use as secondary flower. Stalk length is approximately 30 cm plus.

Leucadendron discolor 'Flame Tip'
Male plants display yellow flowers with red bobbly centres. Most attractive and unusual flowers. Good secondary flower. Flowering time is spring. Stalk length is 20–50 cm.

Leucadendron gandogeri 'Golden Glory'
Female plants display fabulous open creamy-golden flower heads. Secondary or feature flower. Flowering time is late winter/spring. Stalk length is 30 cm plus.

Leucadendron 'Inca Gold'
Female plants produce yellow tulip-shaped flowers. Good secondary flower. Flowering time is autumn/winter. Stalk length is 30 cm plus.

Leucadendron 'Jubilee Crown'
Female plants produce small red cones in spring. Use as a filler flower. Stalk length is 30 cm plus.

Leucadendron laureolum (yellow tulip)
Female plants display yellow tulip-shaped flowers. Good dried flower. Use as a secondary or feature flower. Flowering time is winter. Stalk length is 30 cm plus.

Leucadendron macowanii
Female plants produce burgundy cones during winter/spring. Great dried. Stalk length is 30 cm plus.

Leucadendron 'Maui Sunset'
Female plants produce lovely cream tulip-shaped flowers. Great secondary or feature flower. Flowering time is winter/spring. Stalk length is 30 cm plus.

Leucadendron orientale
Female plants produce large yellow flowers in winter. They are unusual because they turn pink towards the end of spring then produce red cones in summer. Good secondary or feature flower. Stalk length is 60 cm.

Leucadendron 'Safari Sunset'
Female plants produce red tulip-shaped flowers which are good as secondary or feature flowers. Flowering time is autumn/winter. Stalk length is 30 cm plus.

Leucadendron salicifolium
Male plants display sprays of tiny yellow flowers up the stem. Good filler flower. Flowering time is winter. Stalk length is 60 cm to 1 m in length.

Leucadendron 'Silvan Red'
Female plants produce long-lasting red tulip-shaped flowers of medium size. Good fresh or dried. Excellent secondary or feature flower. Stalk length ranges from 30 to 60 cm.

Leucadendron tinctum (rose cockade)
This plant displays yellow flower heads in winter turning to rosy-pink open flower heads with deep rose-pink centres in spring. Good secondary or feature flower. Stalk length is 30 cm plus.

Leucospermum (pincushion protea)

Leucospermum cordifolium 'Caroline'
Round, dark pink, spiky, pincushion flowers. Excellent feature flower. Flowering time is spring; stalk length is 30 cm plus.

Leucospermum cordifolium × pottum 'Firewheel'
Round, spiky flower heads with red centres and orange/red styles. Excellent feature flower. Flowering time is late spring; stalk length is 30 cm plus.

Leucospermum cordifolium 'Sunburst'
Round pincushion flowers displaying yellow centres and red/orange styles. Wonderful feature flower. Flowering time is spring. Stalk length is 30 cm plus.

Leucospermum cordifolium 'Vlaam'
Large, round, orange pincushion flower. Excellent feature flower. Flowers appear in late spring. Stalk length is 30 cm plus.

Leucospermum cordifolium × glabrum 'Selection 52'
Round, orange flowers with pink centres. Excellent medium sized feature flower. Flowers appear in late spring; stalk length 30 cm plus.

Leucospermum lineare × glabrum × cordifolium 'Tango'
Large, red/orange flower heads. Very striking appearance makes it an excellent secondary or feature flower. Flowering time is late spring; in warmer climates flowers appear in winter. Stalk length is 30 cm plus.

Leucospermum tottum (pink star)
Exquisite, delicate pink-tipped flowers with darker pink centres. Wonderful secondary or feature flower. Flowers appear in late spring. Stalk length is 30 cm plus.

Protea compacta (the Prince)
Flower heads are approximately 15 cm in length. Rich pink flowers with deep purple/pink centres. Excellent feature flower. Flowering time is winter/spring. Stalk length is approximately 30–60 cm.

Protea cynaroides (King protea)
This protea produces very large pink flower heads (can be larger than a saucer) with creamy/pink centres. Heavy and dramatic feature flowers. Flowers can be obtained throughout the year using different varieties; the main flowering time is spring. Stalk length is approximately 60 cm.

Protea longifolia (ermine tail)
Long flower heads, approximately 15 cm in length. The flowers are cream-coloured with a dark blackish centre coming to a peak. Good feature flower. Flowering time is winter. Stalk length is 30 cm plus.

Protea longifolia 'Special Pink'
Pink flower heads are approximately 15 cm in length. Great feature flower. Flowering time is winter. Stalk length is 30 cm plus.

Protea magnifica (Queen protea)
Large, dramatic, cream or pink flowers with fluffy cream centres. Interesting feature flowers. Flowering time is late winter/summer. Stalk length is approximately 60 cm.

Protea nerifolia (pink mink)
Pink flower with black beard. A cream-coloured variety with black beard ('white mink') is also available. Excellent feature flower. Flowering time is autumn/winter. Stalk length is approximately 60 cm.

Protea 'Frosted Fire'
Pink flowers with white beards, approximately 15 cm in length. Very popular feature flower. Flowering time is winter. Stalk length is approximately 60 cm.

Protea 'Pink Ice'
All pink flower heads, approximately 15 cm in length. Very popular cut flower. Excellent feature flower. Flowering time is autumn. Stalk length is approximately 60 cm.

Protea repens 'Late Summer'
Pink flowers are approximately 12 cm in length. Lovely feature flower. Flowering time is summer. Stalk length is 30 cm plus.

Protea repens 'Guerna'
Dark red, open flower head, approximately 12 cm in length. Good feature flower. Flowering time is summer. Stalk length is 30 cm plus.

Protea repens 'Honey Glow'
Cream flowers are approximately 12 cm in length. Very popular cut flower and feature flower. Flowering time is autumn/winter. Stalk length is 30 cm plus.

Protea repens 'Ruby Blush'
Pink flowers, approximately 12 cm in length.

Good feature flower. Flowering time is autumn/winter. Stalk length is 30 cm plus.

Serruria florida 'Blushing Bride'

Small cream/pink flowers with fluffy centres. The flowers have a rose-like appearance and are very popular wedding flowers. Good secondary or feature flower. Flowering time is spring. Stalk length is approximately 30 cm.

Serruria florida 'Sugar 'n Spice'

Flowers are similar to 'Blushing Bride' but richer in colour. Flowers have a deep pink interior and paler pink outer petals. Very pretty secondary or feature flower. Flowering time is late winter/spring.

Orchids

Exotic orchids

Lc Irene Finney 'York' (*cattleya* alliance)

A striking lilac orchid with a ruffled burgundy and yellow lip. Feature flower. Flowering time is winter/early spring.

Bc Mount Hood (*cattleya* alliance)

A stunning ruffled pinky-lilac orchid with a yellow throat. Feature flower. Flowering time is autumn.

Cattleya Princess Bells 'Betty's Bouquet'

A dramatic ruffled white orchid with a yellow throat. It is a large standard cattleya which is sought-after as a wedding bouquet flower. Feature flower. Flowering time is winter.

Cattleya Toowong 'Sherwood'

An impressive white orchid with a yellow throat. Perfect as a cut flower. Feature flower. Flowering time is summer.

Blc Zilzie Fry 'Jay Kay' AM AOC (*cattleya* alliance)

A top quality purple cattleya with yellow lips. Feature flower. Flowering time is winter.

Cymbidium Clarisse Austin 'Bimerah'

A lovely pink orchid with yellow lips and maroon markings. Feature flower. Flowering time is spring.

Cymbidium 'Little Sue'

Red flower with red spotted lips and throat. Feature flower. Flowering time is late winter.

Cymbidium Pearl Balkis 'Fiona'

A truly lovely white orchid with a contrasting pale rose-pink lip spotted with crimson. Feature flower. Flowering time is winter to spring.

Cymbidium Rincon 'Clarisse'

White flowers with pale pink stripes and a cream lip which is stunningly marked with crimson. Feature flower. Flowering time is autumn.

Cymbidium Sensation × Betley Radiance

A deep burgundy-coloured orchid with cream lips and rich burgundy markings. Feature flower. Flowering time is spring.

Cymbidium Terama

A pale burgundy-red flower with red and yellow lips. Feature flower. Flowering time is spring.

Cymbidium Wamara × Kerta

Deep pink flower with spotted lips. Feature flower. Flowering time is early winter.

Cymbidium Winter Wonder

Yellowy-green orchid with cream lips and maroon spots. Feature flower. Flowering time is spring.

Cymbidium Winter Wonder 'Jeannie'

A clear green flower with cream lips and maroon spots. Feature flower. Flowering time is spring.

Cymbidium Zuma Boyd × Arcadian Melody

A clear green flower with dark maroon spotted lips. Feature flower. Flowering time is spring.

Dendrobium chrysotoxum

A lovely fragrant golden-yellow orchid which displays a well-rounded lip. The lip is usually a deep orange colour and often shows a maroon disc. Feature flower. Flowering time is spring.

Dendrobium Dalellen 'Baby'

A white orchid touched with lilac. A popular cut flower. Feature flower. Flowering time is autumn.

Dendrobium **Lady Gem Profusion**
This plant displays clusters of mauve orchid flowers. Feature flower. Flowering time is autumn.

Dendrobium **(Singapore orchid)**
Singapore orchids are available in a wide variety of colours and flowers. While available all year as an imported flower, in Australia the main flowering time is summer through to autumn. Very popular cut flower. Feature flower.

Dendrobium wardianum
A truly attractive perfumed white orchid tipped with purple. The lip is brightly coloured in yellow, with two maroon blotches at the base. Feature flower. Flowering time is winter.

Dendrobium williamsonii
Ivory white orchid with an attractively marked lip which is brick red in colour. A fragrant orchid. Feature flower. Flowering time is spring/summer.

Paphiopedilum **(slipper orchid)**

Paphiopedilum **Cameo 'Wyld Court' AM/RHS**
Long stems bear flowers displaying red/brown petals with greenish-white dorsal sepals on the lips which are heavily spotted with red. Feature flower. Flowering time is winter.

Paphiopedilum **Chipmunk 'Vermont' AM/RHS**
Attractive rich green flowers with chocolate/brown markings. Feature flower. Flowering time is winter.

Paphiopedilum **Honey Gorse 'Sunshine' AM/RHS**
A striking yellow/green orchid. Feature flower. Flowering time is winter.

Paphiopedilum **Royale 'Downland' AM/RJS & GMM**
Lovely large flowers are a combination of delicate rose-red shaded with green. Feature flower. Flowering time is winter.

Paphiopedilum **Silvara 'Halo' AM/AOS**
White orchid with splashes of yellow on the petals and a yellow lip. Feature flower. Flowering time is winter.

Phalaeonopsis **Cadiz Rock 'Art Shade'**
Rich pink orchid with red lips. Feature flower. Flowering time is winter/spring.

Phalaenopsis **Queenslander Queen**
A magnificent large white orchid with tiny yellow touches on the lips. Feature flower. Flowering time is winter/spring.

Native Orchids

Cymbidium suave
Slender, hanging spikes are massed with tiny yellow/green orchids. Use spikes as feature flowers. Flowering time is spring.

Dendrobium **'Bardo Rose'**
Small cream-tipped pinky/lilac orchids with softly spotted throats. Use sprays as feature flowers. Flowering time is spring.

Dendrobium bigibbum **'Superbum' 'Col' HCC-AOC (Cooktown orchid)**
This plant bears masses of cerise orchids which resemble Singapore orchids. Feature flowers. Flowering time is autumn.

Dendrobium canaliculatum
Delicate cream-tipped lemon orchids with purple throats. Tiny, long, fairy-like sprays. Use sprays as feature flowers. Flowering time is late winter/spring.

Dendrobium × *delicatum*
Masses of delicate shell-pink orchids forming fine sprays. Sweetly perfumed. Use sprays as feature flowers. Flowering time is late winter/spring.

Dendrobium **'Ellen'**
Delicate shell-pink orchids with faintly spotted tongue. Use sprays as feature flowers. Flowering time is spring.

Dendrobium falcorostrum
Five-petalled, star-like, creamy/white orchids forming pretty sprays. Use sprays as feature flowers. Flowering time is late winter/spring.

Dendrobium × gracilium

Deep yellow orchids forming 30 cm (12'') sprays. Use sprays as feature flowers. Flowering time is late winter/spring.

Dendrobium 'Joy Wray'

Bell-like soft mauve orchids massed on short stems. Use sprays as feature flowers. Flowering time is late winter/spring.

Dendrobium kingianum

Dainty sprays of tiny, mauve/purple orchids. Short stems. Use sprays as feature flowers. Flowering time is spring.

Diuris longifolia (donkey orchid)

Diuris longifolia (donkey orchid)

Called the donkey orchid because the flowers appear to have a face and two upstanding ears. Very dainty and pretty. Brown/yellow with violet chin.

Phalaenopsis amabilis

Large, flat flowers, approximately 5 cm (2'') in diameter, white with a touch of lemon in the centre. Feature flower. Flowering time is variable, between spring and summer.

Pterostylis baptistii

Green/cream striped spider-like orchids. Striking in modern wedding work. Tall, straight upright stem. Feature flower. Flowering time is late winter/spring.

Sarcochilius ceciliae (fairy bells)

Delicate pink or white bell-like orchids on short stems. Feature flower. Flowering time is spring.

Sarcochilius falcatus (orange blossom orchid)

Exquisitely shaped creamy/white orchids with yellow and purple markings. Feature flower. Flowering time is spring.

Sarchochilius fitzgeraldii (ravine orchid)

Pretty orchids borne on slender stems. Creamy/white splashed with soft red.

Note: Flowering times depends on geographical areas.

Foliages and Ferns

Acacia podalyriifolia (Queensland silver wattle)

Valued for its rounded silver-grey leaves and attractive buds. Buds appear in autumn as showy, delicate sprays set against the silver leaves.

Adenanthos obovata (basket flower)

Long, thin, shapely single branches with tiny, oval green leaves covering the stem. Wonderful as outline material as well as for filling in between flowers. Can be dried, changing colour gradually to a deep rich brown. A Western Australian native.

Adiantum capillus veneris (maidenhair fern)

Pretty, fine, scalloped foliage is ideal for bouquets and other wedding work as well as general use. Burn stalk ends after cutting, condition overnight.

Adiantum formosum (black stemmed or giant maidenhair fern)

A magnificent maidenhair growing to 120 cm (4

ft) tall but still retaining a dainty appearance. Can be dried by pressing.

Alocasia
Large glossy green leaves.

Anthurium cordifolium
Large leaves.

Asparagus densiflorus 'Myers' (foxtail fern)
Upright, bushy fern rising to a point.

Asparagus plumosa
Dainty-leaved, long trailing fern frequently used in wedding work and for large, flowing pedestal arrangements.

Aspidistra
Large tapering leaves on long stems can be dried and bleached.

Asplenium nidus (bird's nest fern)
Long, tapering, firm, shiny green leaves. Excellent for modern floristry.

Athertonia diversifolia (blue almond tree)
Large, glossy, dark green leaves measuring up to 15 cm (6'') × 7.5 cm (3''). Useful in modern floristry. Leaves eventually turn rich chocolate brown before crinkling. Can be glycerined.

Baeckea 'La Petite'
Sprays of fine leaves are borne on slender branches.

Baeckea 'Mt Tozer'
Densely packed, tiny, rounded, shiny leaves.

Betula pendula (silver birch)
Dainty pendulous leaves can be glycerined.

Blechnum articulatum
Lovely, tall, erect tropical fern growing to 70 cm. Do not store in very low temperatures.

Blechnum patersonii
A most attractive fern with flat, broad, divided fronds. Grows well in cool, shady situations.

Bowenia serrulata (Byfield fern)
Glossy, serrated, dark to medium green leaves. May be used in one piece where a fan-like appearance is required or individual fronds may be removed from the main stem. Very long stems. Popular cut foliage plant.

Brassaia actinophylla (umbrella tree)
Shiny, bright green leaves, ranging from small to medium size, oval in shape.

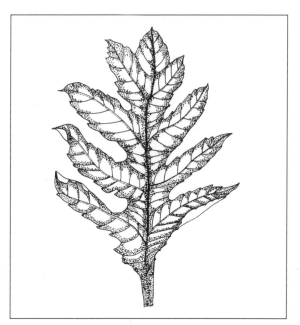

Athertonia diversifolia (blue almond tree)

Brassaia actinophylla (umbrella tree)

Limonium (annual statice)

Limonium (hybrid 'Misty Blue')

Moluccella laevis (Bells of Ireland)

Podocarpus drydougana (emu grass)

Polianthes tuberosa (tuberose)

Phalaenopsis Cadiz Rock 'Art Shade'

Phalaenopsis Queenslander Queen

49

Protea cynaroides (King protea)

Protea grandiceps (Princess protea)

Protea nerifolia (White Mink)

Protea hybrid 'Pink Ice'

Protea magnifica
(Queen protea, pink)

Protea magnifica
(Queen protea, white)

Protea repens (honey protea)

Rosa 'Peter Frankenfield'

50

Rosa 'Mr Lincoln'

Rosa 'Bridal Pink'

Rumohra adiantiformis (leather fern)

Salix caprea (pussy willow)

Sarcochilius ceciliae (fairy bell orchid)

Sarcochilius falcatus (orange blossom orchid)

51

Stirlingia (dried flowers)

Stirlingia (dried buds)

Thryptomene calycinea

Telopea 'Shady Lady' (hybrid waratah)

Verticordia browneii (cauliflower morrison)

Verticordia nitens (golden nitens or nitens morrison)

Zantedeschia elliottiana (calla lily)

Buxus (box)
Masses of tiny, rounded leaves.

Caladium
Large and small multi-coloured leaves. Attractively shaped.

Camellia
Smallish, shiny, crisp dark green leaves.

Callitris rhomboidea (Port Jackson or dune pine)
Dense, fine, pine-like foliage in a pretty shade of green. Graceful and quite magnificent in spring when green foliage is covered in tiny gold buds resembling 'gold dust'.

Callitris rhomboidea (Port Jackson pine)

Codiae variegatum (croton)
This species is valued for its magnificent range of highly coloured red, green, yellow and orange leaves. Very useable leaf size, excellent for mixing with flowers like grevilleas, strelitzias and leucospermums.

Cycas media
Large, stiff, dark green palm leaves. Can be dried.

Darwinia citriodora
Lemon-scented, tightly packed, small leaves and red new growth. Other *Darwinia* species are also valued for their foliage.

Daviesia cordata (bookleaf)
Small to medium-sized broad, tapering leaves which are gum-like in appearance, bearing leafy seed pods. Can be air-dried, glycerined, bleached and/or dyed. A Western Australian native.

Dieffenbachia species
This genus produces a wide range of species with very large to small variegated leaves. Many of the smaller varieties are ideal for modern floristry.

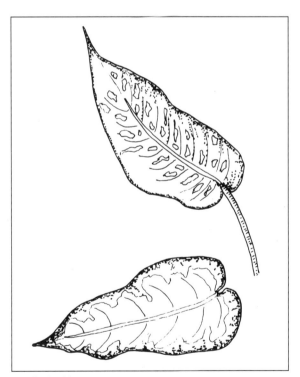

Dieffenbachia

Dracaena species
Variable, large and small leaves; some long and narrow with white stripes. Excellent for modern floristry.

Dracaena

Eremophila species
Tall, straight, single stems are covered in masses of narrow, long leaves. Great as outline material or where interesting texture is required. Will air-dry.

Eucalyptus caesia (gungurru)
Powdery grey stems and foliage.

Eucalyptus cinerea (silver dollar gum or argyle apple)
Silver/green rounded leaves.

Eucalyptus citriodora
Long, dark green leaves are strongly lemon-scented.

Eucalyptus crucis
Silver foliage.

Eucalyptus elata (river peppermint)
Dark green, hanging peppermint-scented leaves.

Eucalyptus gamophylla
Silver foliage.

Eucalyptus globulus (Tasmanian blue gum)
Leaves are covered in powdery blue bloom.

Eucalyptus kruseana (Kruse's mallee)
Small, rounded leaves circling up stem. Sometimes called 'spinning gum'. Frost and

drought resistant. Also resistant to chewing insects.

Eucalyptus macrocarpa (mottlecah)
Silvery/grey foliage.

Eucalyptus maculata
Long, thin, arching, pointed leaves.

Eucalyptus nicholii (willow peppermint)
Graceful, pendulous, blue/grey leaves.

Eucalyptus perriniana (spinning gum)
Silver/green, rounded leaves spiralling up stem.

Eucalyptus pluricaulis
Purple foliage.

Eucalyptus pulverulenta (silver-leafed mountain gum)
Extremely pretty silver leaves.

Eucalyptus rhodantha (rose mallee)
The leaves are an attractive heart shape and are quite large. Silvery/grey in colour.

Eucalyptus sideroxylon
Silver/grey narrow leaves.

Eucalyptus tetragona (tallerack or white-leaved marlock)
Long silver/blue leaves and white square-shaped stems.

Note: Many eucalypts can be dried successfully, particularly the mallee group, 'spinning gums', and those with long narrow leaves. Air-dry or glycerine. They can also be bleached and/or colour dyed.

Genista (broom)
Long, green, string-like stems.

Gleichenia dicarpa (pouched coral fern)
Very fine, multi-branched fish-bone fern. Can be dried.

Grevillea barklyana hybrid form
Light green leaves and pink new growth.

Grevillea hookeriana
Long serrated leaves and long straight stems. Foliage dries to a pretty brown colour. A popular foliage plant.

Grevillea 'Ivanhoe'
Long straight stems and long serrated leaves.

Lauris nobilis (bay laurel)
Leaves can be glycerined.

Leptospermum petersonii (lemon-scented tea tree)
Masses of fine lemon-scented leaves on fine branches. Very popular.

Leucodendron argenteum
Silver foliage.

Leucadendron comicum
Female plants have small silvery-green leaves. Branches can be left to form cones. In spring leaves under the cones turn red.

Leucadendron coniferum
Green foliage can be left to form 'beehive' type rosy cones in late spring/summer.

Leucadendron eucalyptifolium
Long sprays of yellow flowers form during late winter to spring.

Leucadendron laureolum
Female plants provide useful foliage in autumn/winter. The plant features green leaves and green tulip buds which appear at the top of stem in April.

Leucadendron 'Jubilee Crown'
Needle-like foliage. Branches can be left to form small pink cones in spring.

Leucadendron stelligerum
Silver/green fine foliage. Branches can be left to form small yellow cone flowers in spring.

Leucadendron thymifolium
Female plants have small grey leaves close to the stem. Branches can be left to form pink cones in early summer.

Leucadendron utiginosum
Female plants have long silvery foliage throughout the year. Branches can be left to form small yellow flowers in spring.

Lobelia trigonicaulis
Small heart-shaped foliage.

Lycopodium myrtifolium (long club moss or mountain moss)
A dainty fern made up of masses of tiny, coarse branches, giving it an interesting texture. A widely used and sought-after inclusion, particularly in wedding flower arrangements. Will dry, but loses colour.

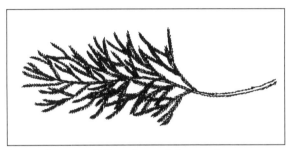

Lycopodium myrtifolium (long club moss)

Lycopodium phlegmaria (coarse or common tassel fern)
There is a wide variety of ferns in this genus which prove useful where long, trailing effects are required.

Magnolia grandiflora (evergreen magnolia)
Large leaves can be glycerined.

Melaleuca species
Fine-leaved species are a good foliage filler.

Nephrolepis exalata (Boston fern)
Long, sweeping, toothed leaves.

Oreocallis wickhamii (North Queensland tree waratah)
Broad, bright green foliage. Good for modern floristry.

Phormium species (New Zealand flax)
Very long, stiff, tapering, slender brown or green or green and white leaves. Excellent for modern floristry.

Pittosporum rhombifolium
Shiny green rich leaves.

Podocarpus drydougana (emu grass)
Long, thin leaves on a long straight stem. Will dry. Very popular greenery.

Ptostrata (scrub leaves)

Extremely attractive, finely-toothed, medium-sized leaves. Outstanding feature leaves. Can be dried and colour dyed.

Rumohra adiantiformis (leather leaf fern)

A widely-used fern which resembles bracken fern.

Salix caprea (pussy willow)

Slender brown stems display buds in winter which can be stripped to reveal fluffy white interiors.

Salix matsudana (tortured willow)

Twisting bare branches in winter.

Sasa fortunei (dwarf bamboo)

Small-growing bamboo.

Sticherus (umbrella fern)

A much used and well-loved fern. Dainty rounds of pointed, divided fronds. Tropical plant which dries out or burns if stored in very cold temperatures. Will dry if pressed.

Templetonia species

Lovely, upright, tall, single stems, sometimes branching out into stem clusters at the top. Can be air-dried.

Xanthorrhoea species (grass tree)

Lovely sprays of slender long stems. Great for adding height or curling. Will dry and can be colour sprayed.

Sticherus gleicheniaceae (umbrella fern)

Xanthorrhoea preissi (grass tree)

3 Pests and Diseases

While we would all like to have pest and disease-free gardens, the truth is that at some stage in our gardening careers we will encounter unfavourable conditions where pest-ridden or diseased plants prevail. Hopefully any problems will be on a small and familiar scale, say the odd caterpillar or two, but sometimes our plants can sustain extensive damage through pests or disease.

Note: In the control of pests and diseases, we may at times have to turn to chemical usage, so a word of caution should be mentioned.

Always maintain the safety of your health when using pesticides and fungicides. Read the labels carefully. Do not mix chemicals together unless they are compatible. Wear protective clothing. Cover all limbs, wear solid shoes (preferably high boots), gloves and a mask. Cover your head. Avoid spraying chemicals on windy days to avoid spray drift. And be aware that not all chemicals are available nationwide.

Warning: Avoid all contact with chemicals if pregnant. Consult your doctor about the chemicals which could be a danger to the foetus if avoidance is not possible.

Pests

Aphids

If the problem is not large, try rubbing these insects off the stems by hand, or hose them off.

If this doesn't work, use soapy water, garlic sprays or non-toxic pyrethrum sprays.

If the infestation is so great that none of these measures have been successful you may need to use Malathion or Rogor chemical sprays. Rogor remains toxic for about one week after use, Malathion for about four days. Do not use Malathion on petunias, sweet peas, ferns, snapdragons and zinnias, or Rogor on asters, chrysanthemums, begonias or gloxinias. Both are ideal for use on roses. Consult your nurseryman expert for individual requirements.

Caterpillars

Where possible pull these pests off the plants by hand and squash. Commercial growers may need to spray using pyrethrum or Bioresmethrin aerosols. If stronger insecticide is required, use Endosulphan (Thiodan). This chemical remains toxic for about one week after use.

The larvae of the moth *Heliothis armigera* are disastrous pests to have on carnation plants. These creatures like to feed firstly on the petal bases of the developing buds then move on to feed on the ovarian tissue. These pests can render a carnation crop unsaleable. Control by spraying with methamidophes (Nitofol).

Eelworm (Nematodes)

This worm-like pest comes in a few varieties, all of which can cause extensive damage. *Aphelenchoides fragariae* attacks anemones, kangaroo paws, bouvardias and some ferns. *Aphelenchoides ritzemabosi* is found mainly on chrysanthemums.

Symptoms of chrysanthemum nematode invasion are blackening of foliage and triangular leaf spots, particularly in the early stages of infection. The disease progresses from lower leaves upwards.

In ferns the main symptom is patchy brown discoloration of the fronds. In extreme cases whole fronds die prematurely.

In all cases to cure the situation try watering the plants with meta-systox. It is a very toxic chemical, so avoid skin contact and inhalation. Lebaycid can also be used. For chrysanthemums specifically, try using demeton-S-methyl, also an extremely toxic substance. Care should be taken by the wearing of rubber gloves, mask and goggles during application.

Another nematode which affects the roots of plants is called *Meloidogyne*. These nematodes cause large swellings or 'galls' on the roots. The galls are often invaded by other organisms which hasten the breakdown of the root system and subsequent collapse of the whole plant. Control by preplant soil treatment with a broad spectrum fumigant or use D-D mixture (Dichloropropane–Dichloropropene) or Di-Trapex. This type of nematode can be a particular problem in carnations and dahlias.

Bulbs may also be attacked by nematodes. Affected bulbs should be destroyed by burning.

Red Spider mite

These tiny fellows can occur in their hundreds on the back of a leaf yet by the naked eye are hard to detect. They thrive in warm, dry conditions. On their diet list are plants like carnations and orchids—cymbidiums seem to be an especial favourite.

Sometimes spraying with soapy water helps but the least toxic and best method of control is to use predatory mites. Speak to your local Department of Agriculture for advice. Otherwise, dust with sulphur or spray wettable sulphur. If the infestation needs harsher chemical treatment

Kelthane, Omite or Rogor can be used. When treating orchids you may want to alternate the use of a systemic insecticide with the chemical Malathion. This treatment should also be of assistance against the pest false spider mite which often attacks *Phalaenopsis* orchids. The best solution is to introduce predatory mites.

Scale

Scale insects can affect roses, orchids, ferns and palms. Brown or soft scale on ferns and palms are best removed by using a soapy cloth and wiping them away. Several kinds of scale insects attack cymbidiums and some other orchids. Treatment should only be carried out when the plant is not flowering. Spray cymbidiums with maldison (Malathion) and white oil. Systemic insecticides can also be particularly useful when treating orchids generally.

Roses can suffer from white scale. Spray with lime-sulphur solution immediately after pruning while plants are dormant. When roses are in growth, paint stems only with this solution or use two tablespoons of white oil with four litres of water and add a teaspoon of Malathion.

Slugs and snails

Where possible, pick these familiar and destructive pests off your plants by hand, otherwise lay baits. Use baits with covers to protect birds and other animals.

Thrips

These small insects attack the foliage and flowers of plants like carnations, roses, gladioli, etc. Spray using Thiodan. This chemical can be alternated with Rogor or Lebaycid.

Diseases

Diseases can be spread by wind passing over infected plants, by implements such as cutting tools (if you suspect a plant of being diseased, tools should be disinfected before use on other plants), by hands and clothes which come into contact with diseased plants, and by insects travelling from plant to plant. Do not take cuttings from diseased plants as you will only be spreading the problem.

Some common disease problems are:

Leaf spots

If not symptomatic of nematode attack, leaf spots are caused by either fungi or bacteria. Spray with Bordeaux for generalised treatment. Where a fungi or bacterial problem is suspected on orchids, cut out the infected area and dust with Dithane powder.

Brown spot occurs especially in *Phalaenopsis* and *Paphiopedilum* orchids. It starts off as a watery area on the leaf surface and if left will rapidly turn brown and spread. Again, cut out the infected area and dust with Dithane powder. If the disease has spread to other plants, also spray with a solution of Natriphene.

Mildew

Mildew appears as grey or white patches on foliage. Powdery mildew presents on the leaves, stems and buds of flowers. It produces an ashy film or spots. Spray with Bordeaux. Downy mildew usually appears under the leaf of the affected plant. Use Bordeaux, Zineb or Mancozeb as a treatment.

Petal blight

This disease appears as brown or transparent flecks on flower petals. Flowers shrivel prematurely and remain attached to the plant. Fungus forms in the petals as 'black seeds', before falling to the ground and developing into mushroom-like growths in the surrounding soil. Spores rise from these mushrooms and float back up to the flower petals, starting the whole process again. Use a systemic fungicide. Also contact fungicides like Mancozeb prove successful if sprayed once a week from bud through to flowering stage. Spray the surrounding ground to get rid of the mushrooms.

Petal blight appears on orchids, often affecting early autumn flowers of *Phalaenopsis* and *Cattleya*. It usually presents as small circular spots on the flowers. The spots are normally dark brown or black with a pink outline. Remove and burn all infected flowers. High humidity encourages the spread of this disease.

Rust

If you see yellow spots on the above side of foliage and circular tan or rust-coloured spots on the underside with a general yellowing of the plant's foliage, pull off the affected plant parts and burn. Spray the remaining plant with Zineb. As a preventative measure, repeat spraying on a monthly basis.

Viruses

Viruses may present in different forms such as malformed buds and flower heads, colour breaks, streaking and variegation in flower colour, or browning and drying off of plants. There is no cure for virus diseases. Remove and burn infected plants.

As a further guide I am now listing some of the more common commercially-grown cut flowers and their diseases.

Warning: Do not take action until the plant disease or pest has been properly identified, preferably by a professional like your local Department of Agriculture advisor.

Carnations

Alternaria leaf spot and branch blight

At first numerous small, dark purple spots appear on younger leaves. These enlarge to form a greyish central area surrounded by a yellowish-green band. A multitude of dark brown fungal spores are evident on the infected areas. Stems may have lesions leading to death of the branch, and in humid weather even the flower buds can be affected, failing to open normally. Spray with Zineb at weekly or fortnightly intervals depending on the severity of the outbreak.

Bacterial leaf and flower blight

This bacterial disease presents as pale brown spots displaying a water-soaked strip on the leaves, stems and calyx of flowers. The spots may form into one large lesion which bands the width of the leaf, stem and calyx. If left unchecked and the infection becomes severe, the leaf will turn yellow and die. Major infection of the calyx will damage the flower inside. There are no effective bactericidal chemicals. Burn affected crops. Sulphur or copper oxychloride sprays can be used as a preventative measure, but with caution due to possible flower damage.

Cladosporium leaf and stem spot

This disease presents as pale brown lesions surrounded with a reddish-purple line. Spray with Zineb.

Septoria leaf spot

This disease presents as light brown to pale grey spots usually surrounded with a purple line. Older spots may show small black dots which are the reproductive structures of the fungus. When spots first appear, spray with copper oxychloride.

Fusarium branch blight

This disease causes rotting of stems and wilting of branches. There is often a pinkish tinge to the rotted area. No chemical treatment is available.

Fusarium wilt

In older plants, branch by individual branch will wilt and die but the young plants tend to yellow first on one side before the leaves wilt. The woody part of the stem is affected, showing a brown stain, and in the last stages the bark rots and falls away. Pre-treat the soil using a soil fumigant such as Di-Trapex. Do not use methyl bromide in soil that is to host carnations.

Phytophthora collar rot

The symptoms of this disease are hard brown rots forming on stem tissue at ground level and wilting foliage. Drench soil with Fongarid, following product directions.

Rhizoctonia collar rot

Open 'sores' on the base of the stem usually have particles of soil adhering to them. A brown discolouration is evident a short way up the stem from the rotting section and the foliage of the plant is wilted. Use Quintozene to drench the soil.

Rust

In its early stages this disease presents as pale grey areas on leaves, stem and calyx of flowers. These patches burst to expose a reddish-brown spore mass. With heavy infection the plant may become stunted and display yellow curling leaves. When the disease first appears sulphur can be used as a spray or dust before flowers open, otherwise flower petals can be marked. Zineb or Oxycarboxin sprays can also be used.

Sclerotium stem rot

The plant will display wilting foliage and will have its stem rotting both at ground level and directly above. The diseased section will be covered with thick, white fungus which contains seed-like bodies, which are first white in colour then turning brown. Drench the soil with Quintozene.

Chrysanthemum

Common rust

Common rust firstly presents as lightly coloured raised spots on the leaves. These spots burst open to display dark brown dusty masses of spores inside. Where there are many spots the leaves will wither. Spray with Zineb or bitertanol (Baycor).

Leaf spot

In the early stages of infection the leaves usually display circular brown spots which then join up to cover most of the leaf. Small, black spots will appear on the dead areas of the leaf. Spray with copper oxychloride or Mancozeb.

Powdery mildew

A white fungus will cover leaves, stems and flower buds. Affected foliage will wither prematurely. Spray using dispersible sulphur.

Ray blight

This fungal disease attacks the flower heads. Small, deep pink spots will appear on the petals. The petals respond by turning light brown to tan before becoming badly rotted. Normally this disease strikes one side of the flower but if badly infected the entire flower head will be affected. The fungus may grow deep into the stem, causing the flower heads to droop and stems to darken. The occasional leaf spot may accompany the disease.

Signs of the disease might not appear until after cutting the flower crop in which case nothing can be done to save the flowers. While plants are still in the ground, first spray with copper oxychloride, then once the flower buds are developing discontinue its use and spray instead with Mancozeb once a week. Spray may cause injury to flowers.

Root rot (Phytophthora)

Symptoms of this disease are yellowing foliage and stem dieback. There is no cure for the disease. Destroy infected crops by burning, then drench the soil with a soil fumigant like Fongarid. Improve soil drainage to prevent further problems.

Spotted wilt

This disease is usually evident by brown, yellow or pale green wavy lines appearing in ring formation on the leaves. Sometimes the flowers are also affected, being of poor shape and quality. This disease is spread by thrips so control these pests with an insecticide such as phorate (Thimet).

Stunt (Chrystanthemum stunt viroid or CSV)

This highly contagious disease spreads quickly via infected sap and cutting tools during handling and cultivation. Not all plants will contract the disease but the ones that do could display mild to severe stunting with mature plants being half to two-thirds their normal size. Symptoms may not be obvious until the plants are flowering. Flowers may be smaller than normal, petals may 'roll in' and the flower buds may form prematurely, opening 7–10 days before buds on healthy plants. Since there is no cure all infected plants should be removed and destroyed. Fumigate the soil with methyl bromide. Do not take cuttings from infected plants.

Verticillium wilt

This disease presents as stunted plants with lower leaves of a pinkish or purplish hue which wither and hang wasted against the stem. There is a more yellow tone to younger leaves and finally the whole plant becomes affected and wilts. Remove and burn all infected plants. Use a soil fumigant like Di-Trapex to drench infected soil.

White rust

The upper surfaces of leaves will be covered with pale green to yellow spots, the centres of which turn brown with age. On the underside of the leaves cream to pink wax-like pustules are formed. As they age, these become almost white in colour. The leaves will distort and wither where there is major infestation. Usually only the leaves are affected but occasionally pustules will also form on flowers, stems and leaf bracts. To treat, cut back all old growth, remove and burn. New growth should be healthy but regularly spray with Tilt, Baycor or Saprol to prevent reinfection.

Dahlias

Collar rot

Wilting of the stem can be caused by dry rot. White fungus harbours white seed-like particles which later turn brown. When transplanting apply Quintozene to the soil as a wettable powder or mix the same amount of dry fungicide throughout the top 10 cm (4'') of soil. Drench the bases of infected plants with the same product.

Crown gall

Bulbous stem adhesions form on the base of the stem on root tubers. Few flowers are produced and the plants are generally spindly or stunted in nature. Destroy and burn affected plants. If planting in infected soil, treat new plants with No-gall before planting.

Leaf spot

A leaf disease displaying small, round, brown spots surrounded with a band. The disease may cause withering and premature leaf death. Spray with copper oxychloride.

Powdery mildew

A white fungus on leaves and stems. Spray with Mancozeb, Thiophanate-methyl or Dinocap. Sulphur can also be used but beware of damaging young foliage and flower heads.

Stem rot

A fungus which usually attacks the stem. Small white 'seeds' turn black as the disease progresses. The plant may wilt and die suddenly. Humidity is a major factor in the progression of the disease. Spray with Dicloran. Be aware that damage can occur to young foliage and flowers.

Spotted wilt

First the leaves display yellow spots or rings which later turn into yellow or brown wavy lines. Sometimes the young stems show brown to purplish streaking. First formed foliage show the clearest symptoms; as the plant matures symptoms are barely noticeable. In very susceptible varieties this virus may turn the leaves brown and the plant may die. Aphids need to be controlled to prevent further spread—use an appropriate insecticide. The dahlias which are most susceptible should be destroyed. Sometimes a small number of cuttings taken from an infected clump can be virus-free and in this way a valuable crop may be saved.

Stunt

The plant takes on a bushy, stunted appearance. Flowers and leaves may be distorted. Symptoms are masked in summer but are clearly noticeable in spring and autumn. Destroy and burn all infected plants.

Gypsophila

Gypsophila can be affected by root rots, crown gall and viruses. They are also prone to a number of fungal diseases, the worst being:

Botrytis

Seedlings, flowers and stems are affected by this disease. Browning of the flower heads occurs, making them unacceptable for sale. Spray with Rovral, Mancozeb or Ronilan. Apply before planting or just after sowing.

Limonium

Botrytis cinerea

Botrytis is spread by airborne spores and attacks seeds, seedlings, flowers, flower stalks, foliage, and even the crowns and stubs left after picking. The disease can present as lesions on stem nodes and dry rot of the crown of the plants, as well as blighted flower heads and shattering of the flowers when picked. Help prevent the disease by reducing humidity. Remove severely diseased flowers and plants from the field and burn. To control this disease spray with Mancozeb, Rovral, Saprol or Ronilan. These chemicals must enter the flower head and penetrate into the hollow flower stalk stubs.

Protea

Armillaria 'Collar rot'

Armillaria 'Collar rot' is a fungal disease which affects proteas, exotics and native trees and shrubs. Similar to root rot diseases, Armillaria causes a slow decline and eventual death of the plant. Symptoms are basal trunk or stem rot and white or creamy-coloured fungal growths which exude a mushroom smell. Look at the bark of the plant for signs of infection. Clumps of mushrooms may be produced at the base of diseased plants throughout the year.

Plants left in pots too long before planting out can produce a poorly developed and twisted root system which is particularly susceptible to this disease.

As there are no fungicides that control the disease, the only option to the grower is to dig out and burn affected plants and leave the ground fallow. Before replanting fumigate the soil using methyl bromide. Please note that methyl bromide is highly toxic and should be applied by professionals. Also note that fumigation of the soil is not always successful.

Roses

Anthracnose

Sometimes young green stems and flowers are attacked but mostly this disease presents on the leaves in the form of small, round black spots with a well defined border. As they get bigger the spots can turn an ash grey colour and fall away leaving the border distinct. There is some yellowing of the leaves around the spots but not a lot of leaf loss. Spray with copper oxychloride.

Black spot

Black spots with shaggy surrounds appear on the leaves. Heavily infected leaves turn yellow and fall from the plant. New growth may also be infected. During humid and warm conditions, spray with a fungicide such as Thiram or Mancozeb.

Canker and dieback

Red and pale yellow spots appear on the bark, gradually increasing in size and turning brown in colour. The bark can develop deep cracks which harbour tiny black dots. In susceptible plants the canker travels down the stem killing the plant. In less susceptible varieties, this disease can be checked. Using a slanting cut, remove affected canes below the diseased area and above a healthy bud.

Downy mildew

This fungal disease can affect the entire plant. Leaves display purplish-red to dark brown irregular spots. Humid weather produces a fungal growth on the undersides of the leaves alongside the spots. Newer leaves will droop and fall off the stems easily. On the stems and flower stalks there is a display of purple spots, streaks and blotches.

With major infections young shoots will die back. Flowers display purplish-brown spots on the calyx and show dead brown areas on the petals. Infected flower buds can cause deformed flowers.

Spray with Zineb or copper oxychloride when symptoms first appear. Two fungicides can be mixed for greater efficacy. Cover the undersides of leaves and stems with spray.

Grey mould and petal spot *(Botrytis cinerea)*

This disease affects the actual rose flowers by firstly turning the flower buds brown and causing them to rot. Where there are flowers partially opened the petals also turn brown and shrivel. On fully-opened flowers ring-like markings appear on the petals. In pale coloured roses these are normally reddish in colour whilst on dark varieties they are light coloured. The disease also presents as a furry, grey fungus growth. Spray with a fungicide like Iprodione, Mancozeb or Dicloran.

Powdery mildew

A powdery, white fungus appearing on leaves, flower stems and buds. Young growth is distorted. Spray with Mancozeb, dinocap or similar. Sulphur can also be used but care must be taken as marking of flower petals can occur.

Rust

This disease is prevalent in spring and summer. Bright-orange powdery spots appear on the backs of leaves, towards the end of summer these turn dark brown and contain black spores. The upper sides of leaves infected with this disease become spotted with yellow markings and leaves may fall prematurely. Spray with Zineb or Oxycarboxin or dust with sulphur.

Conclusion

Of course many other plants could be mentioned, however this section is meant as a guide only. Reputable suppliers of cut flower plant stock will supply all growing and disease and pest information with the purchase of plants.

It must be stressed again that before drastic action is taken, correct identification of the pest or disease problem should be undertaken. You will find your local Department of Agriculture a great help and source of information.

4 Cutting and Storing Flowers and Foliages

There can be nothing more satisfying for the home gardener than to pick flowers and foliages for indoor use which have been grown in their own garden. Of course the longer these cut flowers and foliages last, the longer gardeners can enjoy the fruits of their labours. And so too it is important for the commercial grower to have their 'produce' last. But is there a secret to maintaining the longevity of cut flowers and foliages?

Regardless of their ultimate use, the way in which flowers and foliages are picked and stored, will influence their cut flower life. This section discusses the ways in which flowers and foliages generally—regardless of how they are ultimately used—can be preserved and prolonged. The information is relevant to all types of flowers and foliages.

Picking Flowers and Foliages

The best time to pick flowers is very early morning or late evening, when the temperature is lowest, and the flowers have a high moisture content in their stems. If you are a home gardener wanting to create a flower arrangement, it is wise to have an idea of the arrangement in which the flowers will be used before cutting to prevent waste.

To maintain cut flower longevity and quality, immediately place the flowers or foliages in a bucket of water in a cool, shady location until picking is finished. This helps prevent trauma associated with excessive moisture evaporation. Never lay them down out of water in the sun.

Woody-stemmed plants (e.g. thryptomene, Geraldton wax, lilacs and roses) have in the past often had their stems hammered at the ends after picking, with the idea that splitting them would increase their ability to absorb water. Information from overseas experts now discourages this practice. Bashing and splitting stems damages the water-carrying vessels and inhibits water absorption.

The best method of preserving woody stemmed varieties is to cut or re-cut stems on an angle, approximately 5 cm (2'') from the bottom, under fresh warm water. Warm water is preferred to cold because warm water contains less air, minimising air embolism (air blockage problems). Warm water is also absorbed more quickly by stems than cold water.

To further minimise damage to stem water-carrying vessels, use a very sharp pair of secateurs or other cutting instrument to cut the stems.

When sorting the picked plant material, remove excess foliage from the bottom of the stems and place stems in tepid water. They should stay in water preferably 8–12 hours before transporting or arranging so they can become 'conditioned', i.e. so their stems fill with water and are firm and ready for use. Small ferns may be floated in a tray of water, rather than stood in a bucket. Make sure all containers used are *clean*. This is critical.

Water

Whether you are storing cut flowers and foliages commercially or arranging them at home, the quality of water used is critical to the length of their vase life.

This applies not only to the water in which the plant materials are standing but also to the amount of water in the surrounding atmosphere. The lower the humidity, the more water will be drawn from the flower's surface, leading to drying and wilting of the petals.

It is quite common commercially to see bunches of flowers on display in plastic sleeves. The sleeves retain a high level of humidity around the enclosed flowers. Moisture can also build up on the inside of the sleeve without coming into contact with individual flower petals—a bonus for water-sensitive species.

Sleeves also help protect flowers from the effects of ethylene gas (see page 69).

It cannot be too often stressed that all containers used for cut flowers and foliages must be scrupulously clean. Before use, always scrub the containers with water to which a few drops of bleach have been added, and rinse with fresh water.

To help keep stems and water free of damaging bacterial growth add a few drops of chlorine (household) bleach per 1 litre of water to all buckets and containers, including vases, in which plant material will be stored. This solution should be changed every couple of days as the antibacterial effect weakens after this time. Also remove any foliage or flowers which will sit below the water line.

The amount of bacteria forming in the container water can also be controlled by acidifying the water to a pH level of 3.2 to 3.5. Acidified water is more readily absorbed by cut stems than alkaline water, which has a high mineral content.

An easy way to acidify alkaline water is to add citric acid, obtainable from most pharmacies. Use in quantities of 2.5 g of citric acid to 9 litres of water. Many commercial vase or holding solu-tions contain citric acid as well as antibacterial agents and some protein (sugar). These may be used instead, following packet directions carefully.

The use of rainwater or deionised water in areas where town or dam water is heavily alkaline is recommended.

Recent NSW Department of Agriculture findings suggest that generally fluoride is toxic to gerberas, gladioli and freesias while sodium adversely affects roses and carnations.

Holding Solution

This is the term given to the water solution in which your flowers and foliages will stand, awaiting use. The following recipe is suitable for home and commercial use and can be used in vases as well as holding containers.

9 litres of water (approx. 2 gallons)
2–3 drops of chlorine (household) bleach
2.5 grams (¼ teaspoon) citric acid
80 grams (3½ oz) sugar

An ordinary household bucket holds this quantity. Quantities can be reduced or increased propor-tionally although for vase use, retain the listed amount of chlorine.

Air Blocks

Flowers which have been out of water, even for a short period of time, may suffer from air blocks (air embolism), which means that even if you then stand them in water, the air previously sucked up the stem prevents water being absorbed and the flowers die.

Air blocks may also occur in flowers which contain large amounts of sap. The sap seals over the cut ends, preventing water uptake.

Whichever is the case, it is important to re-cut the stems of flowers and foliages which have been out of water for any period of time. Cut the stems about 2.5 cm (1'') – 5 cm (2'') from the end. The cut should be made on an angle so that when the stems are sitting in a bucket or container, the stem ends are not pressed flat against the base. It is preferable to re-cut stems under running tap water. The stems are then placed in a bucket of tepid water for storage. If you suspect that your flowers have an air blockage (because their heads are drooping) warm water will rise through the stem more quickly than cold.

Conditioning Wilted or Stressed Flowers

'Conditioning' is a term used when speaking of restoring flowers and foliages to good condition. Conditioning is carried out on plant material which has been picked and left out of water too long or picked in too high a temperature.

The time involved in conditioning wilted or stressed flowers and foliages varies, depending on the species and the amount of deterioration. Some plant material may be so far gone that no amount of effort will bring it back. The best results are achieved by using a conditioning solution in conjunction with a coolroom, however if this is not possible use the following recipe and stand your container of plant material in the coolest part of your premises.

Conditioning solution (do not add sugar)

   9 litres of warm water (not hot) (approx. 2 gallons)
   2–3 drops of chlorine (household) bleach
   2.5 grams (¼ teaspoon) citric acid

An ordinary household bucket will hold this quantity which can be reduced or increased

proportionally. Remember to re-cut the stems before placing them in the solution. It could be 24 hours before conditioning takes effect.

After conditioning, store the plant material in a holding solution until use.

Bud Opening Techniques

Sometimes flowers are harvested in tight bud. Gladioli is a good example of this. They are often picked when only one or two florets have bloomed.

To help flowers picked in bud to 'force bloom', re-cut the stems and stand in very warm water with a few drops of bleach added and 10 grams (one teaspoon) of sugar to 1 litre (1¾ pints) of water. A plastic bag pulled over the flower heads and tied at the neck will increase the temperature and assist the buds to open.

Storing Sap-Containing Flowers and Foliages

While most flowers can be stored with others, there are some species which should always be stored on their own. If you are storing flowers like daffodils and jonquils which contain a milky sap, keep them separate from other flowers until their stems stop oozing—usually about six hours. Also try to avoid using them in flower arrangements until all signs of sap have gone. If they are re-cut after the sap has dried, they should be kept separate for a further six hours.

This also applies to those sap-containing foliages like frangipani.

Alstromeria and Dermatitis

While probably more applicable to the commercial user because of the quantity of flowers used, the home gardener should still take heed of the following warning.

Alstromeria flowers are suspected of causing a high incidence of skin problems among regular handlers. Research conducted in the USA indicates repeated skin contact with sap exuded from cut stems causes allergic reactions. Allergic reactions from alstromeria do not seem to occur through casual contact with the flower ends, only through prolonged and repeated exposure.

Symptoms to watch out for include cracking skin, bleeding skin, blistering, itchy, dry or peeling skin, redness or swelling. Once sensitisation has occurred other chemicals or allergens, unrelated to the alstromeria, may set off similar symptoms.

Handlers must take all precautions possible to avoid becoming sensitised in the first place. Precautions include wearing gloves when handling alstromeria, using a sealant such as Vaseline on the hands during contact, storing alstromeria apart from other flowers to avoid sap contamination, even cleaning alstromeria storage containers separately from other plant containers.

It has been found that alstromeria sap remains in the bucket even if the water from that bucket has been tossed out. On refilling the bucket the sap mixes with the fresh water, coating the stems of the next bunch of flowers or foliage. Scrupulously cleaning buckets (wearing gloves) with a scrubbing brush using clean water containing bleach, then tossing that water away and refilling the bucket is a positive way of preventing allergy problems.

Allergy problems have also been associated with other bulb flowers such as tulips, hyacinths, jonquils and daffodils, and some shrub flowers like grevilleas.

Ethylene Contamination

Ethylene is a naturally occurring gas produced by plants, ripening fruit and vegetables; it is also present in some car and machinery exhaust fumes and cigarette smoke—and it is detrimental to cut flower and foliage life.

Because diseased, bruised, rotting or dying foliage and plant materials produce ethylene, it is important to keep cut flower and foliage storage areas clean. Also remove all dead or dying leaves and flower heads from freshly stored stems. If material is to be stored for more than one day, maintain daily checks, removing dying leaves and flowers. Flower arrangements and vased flowers should also be checked regularly.

Experiments are being carried out on certain flowers to minimise the production of ethylene. One flower in particular is the carnation. Some professional cut flower growers are now treating carnations with silver thiosulphate (STS) in solution form to help combat flower losses due to ethylene gas contamination. STS inhibits the natural production of ethylene in the treated flower and also builds into that flower resistance to outside sources of contamination. STS is currently being tested on other flowers.

The use of STS appears to herald a breakthrough in retaining the quality of cut flowers and foliages, but it must be remembered that it works in combination with, not in place of, other conditioning and storage precautions.

Another factor in reducing ethylene contamination is to avoid overcrowding, and thereby overheating, cut flowers and foliages. The hotter a flower becomes, the more ethylene it produces.

Even in a coolroom, some flowers remain more ethylene sensitive than others, so they should be stored as far away from the potential source of contamination as possible.

Others are sure to be added to the list, but at the moment the most commonly known ethylene sensitive flowers are liliums, carnations, Geraldton wax, irises, stocks, orchids (except dendrobiums), alstromeria, delphiniums, freesias, snapdragons and gypsophila (baby's breath). If you are a commercial user, consider sleeving these flowers while storing for added protection.

Temperature and Storage for Commercial Users

Low temperatures surrounding cut flowers and foliages not only decreases their potential for ethylene production but also slows down the process of flower respiration (breathing).

When a flower or foliage is cut, it is removed from further access to energy (carbohydrates). Once the carbohydrates it has at the time of cutting are used up, deterioration takes place until finally the plant material must die. The hotter it is, the faster a flower or piece of foliage breathes. The faster the breathing, the more energy and carbohydrates are used up and the quicker the plant material dies. Cooling slows down the respiration rate and in turn increases the cut flower and foliage life.

While cooling does extend or preserve the life of the plant material, there comes a point where over-cooling occurs. This is a particular problem with flowers—they may look great in the coolroom but then may die within one or two hours of removal.

Different flower species and foliages have different life spans. Many remain in perfect condition for five to ten days in a coolroom; others may last longer, some less.

The temperature you decide to set your coolroom will depend upon the flower or flowers and greenery you are growing and storing.

There is some dissention between coolroom manufacturers and various flower experts over the exact temperature at which each species should be stored but the following list should serve as a guideline.

Suggested Coolroom Storage Temperatures	Flower Species
0–5°C 32–41°F	Bouvardia, carnations, muscari, irises, freesias and most other bulbs, chrysanthemums, roses, daisies, gypsophila, snapdragons, Geraldton wax, banksias, kangaroo paws, proteas, leucadendrons, waratahs, leptospermums, heaths, ericas, boronias, most greenery (excluding tropical ferns which may dry and become brittle). Other flowers similar in type and background to above.
4°C 38°F	Said to be the ideal temperature for storing gladioli, however they are sometimes stored at slightly lower temperatures.
8–10°C 44–50°F	Cymbidium, cattleya and other cool–moderate temperature-growing orchids.
12–15°C 54–59°F	Any sub-tropical or tropically grown flowers or ferns, e.g. vanda orchids, some dendrobiums, particularly Singapore orchids, phalaenopsis orchids, anthurium lilies, strelitzia, sticherus (umbrella fern), maidenhair fern, etc.

Flowers and foliages in the above category usually last well for several days in a room or packing shed as long as the surrounding atmosphere is high in humidity (not heat). Sleeve flowers to assist with this.

As a general rule, the lower end of the preferred temperature scale for each flower group will give the maximum cut flower and foliage life.

Some flower groups survive at slightly lower temperatures than those suggested here, but may have their cut flower life shortened. Conducting your own research before storing large quantities of flowers at alternative temperatures is highly recommended. This applies particularly to anthurium lilies, which are extremely cold sensitive.

5 Drying Cut Flowers and Foliages

The art of drying flowers and foliage has been practised for many years and in today's rushed society provides a logical answer for busy people who wish to decorate their homes with low maintenance floral arrangements. Not everyone has the time to top up water levels in fresh floral displays.

Dried flowers and foliage are easy to look after. Just keep them out of direct sunlight to prevent the colours fading and give them the occasional clean by blowing the dust away with the nozzle of a vacuum cleaner. Your arrangements should keep their looks for at least two years.

Of course there are many other rewards to be gained from using dried flowers and foliage. Arranged in bowls, vases or baskets, or used to highlight novelty gift items such as wall brooms, coat hangers and kitchen spice ropes, dried flowers and foliage bring a special rustic charm to the home.

For the hobbyist, the techniques employed to dry flowers and foliages can be in themselves rewarding. Skill in timing plays a large part and can give a sense of personal satisfaction when the task has been well done.

But what can be the most rewarding of all are those fresh flower arrangements which can be left to dry on their own. This way the beauty of living flowers can be first enjoyed combined with the delight of seeing the arrangement turn into an everlasting decoration.

Commercial flower growers will find a selling bonus using dried flowers and foliages. Fresh flower losses can mount up so growing flowers which can be dried can provide a back up to sales.

Whatever your reason, the interest in dried flowers and foliages is increasing.

In this chapter I will describe the most commonly dried flowers and foliages and explain the various methods employed to gain a professional finish. There are probably many flowers and foliages with the potential for drying which are yet to be discovered. I trust that this chapter will make you, the reader, enthusiastic enough to do your own research and experiments.

Topiary tree using dried flowers

When To Pick

Pick flowers and foliages on a dry day, after the dew has dried from the plant's surface. Because you wish these flowers and foliages to be preserved indefinitely, always pick perfect and unblemished material. Foliage that is to be glycerined should be mature but not dying. Young or dying foliage is inefficient at drawing up moisture.

Helichrysum (everlasting daisies) should be picked in bud or with only one set of petals opened if you do not wish the centres to become exposed. They keep developing even after they have been picked. If you do pick at a slightly more advanced stage, allow the flowers to open indoors to prevent them being pollinated by insects and dropping seeds.

Pick hydrangeas when they begin to fade and the colour starts to turn. Lavender should be picked when the first florets have opened. Roses, which are to be air-dried, should be picked in bud or just as the buds are opening.

You may also want to try something a little different. Allow some of your flowers to go to seed and then collect the seed pods. Alstromeria is one to try and so are the flower-like seed pods formed by onion and garlic plants. Why not use the leftover stems from agapanthus when the florets have fallen off? These are stunning accompaniments to arrangements.

How To Dry Your Plant Material

There are a variety of substances and methods available for drying plants. The choice is usually a matter of personal preference and experimentation. The most commonly used method is air-drying, whereby plant material is hung upside down to dry. However, this is definitely not the only way to dry flowers and foliages. Desiccants (drying agents) such as borax powder, silica gel or sand can be used. When supple foliage is required, glycerine would be the choice. Other methods of preservation such as freeze drying, pressing leaves and flowers and even ironing ferns have their place. Let's have a closer look at each of these methods.

Air-drying

A wide variety of plant materials can be successfully air-dried. Most popular are seed pods, grasses and grains, berry branches, papery flowers, Australian and South African natives, as well as some European flowers like delphiniums and rosebuds.

When you have chosen your materials for drying, strip the stem of as many leaves as possible (unless of course you are drying foliages only) to speed up the process and tie stems together loosely in a bunch. Leave a trail of string long enough to tie over a hook or rafter. Make sure the room, shed or cupboard where these plant materials are to be dried is airy and dark enough to preserve the colours of your plant materials. For this reason do not hang plant materials in direct sunlight.

Hanging flowers upside down in this manner allows the moisture contained naturally within the stem to run down towards the flower head and in most cases the stems of the dried product will become brittle. This is not always obvious in plants such as *Leptospermum* (teatree) or in banksias or proteas as they have naturally very woody stems, but as a general rule drying out of the stems indicates that the material has finished drying. This method can take 7–21 days, so it is a good idea to check your drying area regularly.

Some flowers will air-dry just as well in an upright position compared to hanging upside down—for example banksias and proteas—but care must be taken that the stems do not bend over the edge of the container during the drying process as the stems may assume a curved angle.

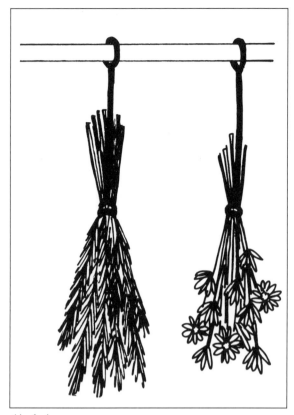

Air-drying

Brittle stems can become a problem in some flowers which you may wish to later wire on a false stem after drying. *Helichrysum* (everlasting daisy) is one example. Not only does the stem become brittle, but the flower head itself becomes hard, making it almost impossible to pass a wire through.

From personal experience I have found the best method of wiring these flowers is not by the traditional hook method. Instead, while the flower is fresh, cut away the stalk leaving a small stub about 1.25 cm (½″) below the flower head. Take a wire, usually 0.71 mm (22 gauge) and push the wire up through the stalk stub and into the flower head. Make sure the wire end is not visible amongst the petals. As it dries, the flower head will shrink onto the wire making gluing unnecessary. I then stand the wired daisies in groups in drinking glasses and store in a dark cupboard to dry.

Generally, in any air-drying process, if flower heads have become crushed or squashed whilst drying, hold them over a steaming kettle and the situation should reverse. Do not be surprised if during this you see flowers like *Helichrysum* or *Ixodia* (South Australian daisy) petals close due to the moisture. Putting them out in the sun for up to an hour to dry off will cause the petals to reopen.

Once the plant materials are thoroughly air-dried they may be stored either by leaving them hanging up or wrapping individual bunches in butcher's paper and standing in a basket or other container which is kept away from mice and sunlight.

Grasses and seed pods can be sprayed with hairspray to keep them from 'falling'.

Desiccants

Desiccants—a health warning

Silica gel, perlite aggregate and other powders are hazardous to your health, so always wear a face mask when working with these materials to avoid inhalation.

Desiccants is the term applied to substances which withdraw moisture. Plant materials can be buried in these and sealed in an airtight container. Over a varying period of time (according to the type of plant being dried) preservation occurs and in most cases the original colour of the flower or foliage is retained.

Silica gel

Flowers like orchids, zinnias, dahlias, roses and bulb flowers respond well to silica gel as does made up work like corsages. Silica gel is a popular medium because it quickly dries materials— usually within 48–72 hours. However, it is very expensive and can leave the flowers fragile. Like any other desiccant, make sure that the silica gel is 100% dry before use.

When purchasing silica gel from your chemist, make sure that it is self-indicating. When silica gel is fresh, dry and ready for use, it will be blue in colour. If it has turned pink, you will need to place the silica gel in a shallow tray and put it into an oven heated to 130°C (250°F) to dry out, once again turning blue. Silica gel can be used over and over again by drying it out in this manner, but remember to always allow it to cool before use. Keep it stored in an airtight container when not in use.

To dry flat-faced flowers such as daisies where you may wish to retain the flower's original stem, choose an airtight container in which you are able to fit a 'shelf'. This shelf can be made from materials such as polystyrene or even cardboard covered with foil, but it must be thin enough to allow you to make a hole large enough for the stem to pass through. The flower head will lie flat upon the shelf, and the stem will hang down through the hole, in its natural position (see diagram).

Pour the silica gel all over the flower, even under and between the petals, until the flower head is completely covered. Depending upon the size of your container you may be able to dry several flowers at once. Seal the container and leave until dehydration has taken place.

If you do not wish to save the stems, pour about 2.5 cm (1'') of silica gel into the bottom of an airtight container (containers like biscuit and cake tins are good), place flower heads flat and face up on the gel, so that no petals are touching then cover petals as before with more silica gel. Seal and store. Afterwards, if you wish to wire with a false stem, use 0.71 mm (22 gauge) wire using the 'hook' method. Then cover with florist tape (Parafilm). (See diagram.)

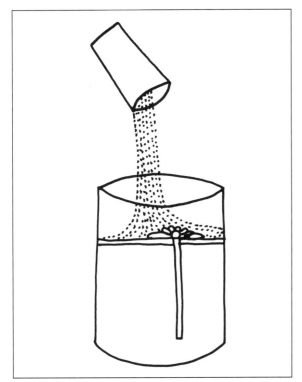

Drying flat-faced flowers in an airtight container with a false shelf

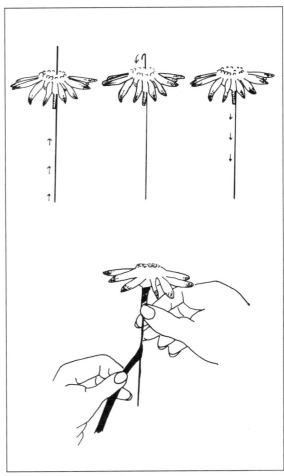

Wiring flowers using the hook method

Flowers like roses and bulb flowers can be dried lengthwise on top of the silica gel. Place 2.5 cm (1'') of silica gel on the bottom of the container. Lay the flower lengthwise on top then cover completely with more silica gel. Seal and store.

Try something different! Pull the petals of a carnation out of the calyx and dry the calyx and stem. You will be left with a mini green tulip! Or pull the petals off a daisy and dry the fluffy centres and stem. These make unusual additions to a mix of dried flowers.

Since silica gel can be a heavy desiccant, very delicate flowers may be better preserved using borax powder or perlite aggregate.

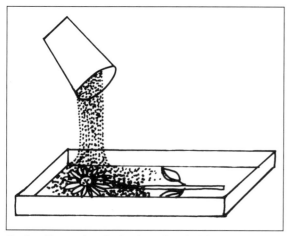

Drying flowers lengthwise in a flat airtight container

Borax powder and perlite aggregate

Flowers which can be dried using silica gel can also be dried using borax powder and perlite aggregate but the drying time is longer.

Borax powder is available from hardware stores and some chemists. Perlite aggregate can be purchased from building suppliers.

Borax powder is a very finely textured powder and care must be taken to make sure that all of the plant material is covered. It also has the habit of sticking to the surface of the drying material. Be prepared to brush away any powder from the petals or leaves, using a small artist's brush, upon removal of dried material from the drying box.

The principle for drying materials with powders is the same as for drying with silica gel, except for the timing factor. Allow roughly 7–10 days (sometimes much longer). If you're not sure whether the plant material is ready, brush the desiccant aside, inspect and touch the petals. If the material is crisp, the procedure is finished. If the plant still feels 'alive', cover with powder again and reseal. Take another look a day or so later.

Borax can be used on its own, or if a heavier substance is needed mix two parts borax to one part sand.

Borax powder and perlite aggregate can be dried in the oven after use and stored. See section on silica gel and copy.

Sand

Builders' sand can be used but it should be washed beforehand to remove any impurities. To wash, place it in a bucket until it is three-quarters full. Fill the remainder of the bucket with water. Stir with your hand to dislodge any debris and then allow the water to settle before scooping off the surface. Do this several times with clean water and then dry the sand in a warm oven 130°C (250°F) for several hours. Put it through a sieve before use.

If all this is a bit much, preferably use fine silver sand. This doesn't need washing, only drying in the oven as described above. Use an enamel bowl or metal tray.

Sand is very heavy so it is not suitable for very delicate flowers. Try it on flowers like roses, daisies, tulips and other medium weight flowers.

If the surrounding temperature is warm, sand can be used uncovered. Flat-faced flowers like daisies are placed face down on a tray filled with about 2.5 cm (1'') of sand. Their stalks can be sticking upright. Cover with more sand by trickling it over the petals.

Other flowers like roses can be laid sideways on the sand. To cover flowers a spoon is used. Fill with sand then shake contents gently over the flowers to be dried. Flowers with open throats like daffodils should have their cavities filled with sand.

To avoid post treatment shrivelling of flowers make sure they are completely dried before removing from the sand. It may take at least 14 days before the drying process is completed. If in doubt, wipe some of the sand from the petals, feel them, and if not dried, replace with more sand and wait a few more days before checking again.

Tip for using desiccants

If petals on any of the dried flowers look wrinkled, try using a heavier desiccant like sand next time so the petals will be 'ironed out'.

Glycerining

Glycerine can be purchased from chemists. The usual dilution is one part glycerine to two parts boiling water. Stir the glycerine and water to mix thoroughly. If desired this can be done in a saucepan on the stove. If you find this strength solution doesn't work, you may wish to try a stronger solution. In this case 50% glycerine to 50% water is recommended.

Glycerining is the ideal method for preserving foliage and is rarely used for flowers (*Thryptomene calycina* is one exception which comes to mind). Bracken fern, *Eucalyptus cinerea* (silver dollar gum), *Magnolia grandiflora* and ivy respond well and these and other glycerined foliage take on a supple and life-like appearance when treated.

The procedure is relatively simple. Cut the stems of the plant to be treated on an angle under warm running water to remove any air embolism and then stand in about 10–15 cm (4–6'') of solution. The solution can still be hot when used. Leave in a cool, dark, dry place until the leaves have absorbed the solution. Do not forget—pick foliage in its prime for best results, not too young

nor too old. You may need to top up the fluid level from time to time.

Individual leaves such as *Oreocallis wickhami* (North Queensland tree waratah) may be glycerined by placing the solution in a shallow dish and totally immersing the leaves until they change colour. Glycerined leaves usually turn dark brown or grey. *Pittosporum rhombifolium* (diamond laurel) and the leaves from *Athertonia diversifolia* (blue almond tree) also respond well to glycerining. In fact with investigation, I am sure you will find many foliages which dry successfully.

Whichever leaves you do choose to treat in this manner, once the colour change has occurred, remove them from the tray, gently wash them in clean water, removing any excess glycerine, then place them on blotting paper to dry.

Glycerining foliage or individual leaves can take anything from one week to ten weeks—two to three weeks being the average drying time. Again, the timing for different species varies. Also the actual texture of the plant material influences the timing. The thicker and firmer the leaf, the more glycerining time should be allowed.

If you wish to speed things up, wipe the leaves of the branch individually with the solution before standing the stems in it.

Over-glycerining—when the leaves start to drip glycerine—can be a problem. So, the best thing is to keep a regular watch. When there is no obvious distinction between un-glycerined leaves and treated ones, you know the plant material is ready. Feel the underside of the leaves. If they are slightly greasy to the touch, this too indicates it is time to remove the stems from the glycerine.

If you have left the material too long in the glycerine and your leaves are dripping, try to wipe as much solution from them as possible and stand them in a dry place. Watch for mildew. This can be removed with soapy water.

If the glycerining process has obviously been completed but your leaves are crispy around the edges, hang your treated material upside down for a few days to allow the glycerine solution in the plant to move to the tips of the leaves.

You can store leftover glycerine solution by

adding approximately ¼ - ½ teaspoon of bleach to ½ litre (1 pint) of glycerine solution to discourage the formation of mildew.

Water Drying

Some dried arrangements are simply made by allowing plant materials to dry as they stand in their containers. The material is left to stand in water-soaked oasis or is picked and placed in a vase containing about 5 cm (2'') of water. As the water evaporates so too will the arrangements begin to dry. Australian natives, South African plants, some ferns and mature hydrangeas will dry in this way.

Tip: how to dry hydrangeas

The important factor in successfully drying hydrangeas is in timing the picking. As stated earlier in this chapter, it is important to pick hydrangeas as they mature, that is, when their colour turns. Remove all but a few leaves. Cut and place in 2.5 cm–5 cm (1''–2'') of water. Do not top the water level up, rather allow the water to evaporate. Your hydrangeas should dry perfectly in this fashion. Some people air-dry hydrangeas and occasionally some people glycerine them.

Microwave Oven Drying

Microwave drying your flowers can be fun. A relatively modern way of drying flowers, it is still open to a lot of experimentation to determine just which flowers are suitable and how long they take to dry. For example, some successful choices are carnations, daisies and daffodils; some trickier ones are magnolias and dahlias. Colours of flowers can change too although this is not always the case. Yellow flowers stay yellow while white flowers can take on a grey tinge and blue flowers can turn purple. Underdeveloped flowers dry more successfully than full blown flowers, which may drop their petals. Following are two different microwaving techniques to choose from:

1. Put 5 cm (2'') of kitty litter into a microwave-proof container (the kitty litter acts as a desiccant). Place the flowers face up, spacing them evenly in the litter so the petals aren't touching. The shortened flower stems will be pushed down into the kitty litter. Let them rest on the litter and then cover their petals completely with more kitty litter.

You may make up one or more containers of flowers and place them on the turntable towards the centre of your microwave. Now place 1 cup of water on the back of the turntable. Put the heat on high for 30 seconds to 3½ minutes. Start at the low end of the time scale.

Allow the flowers to remain covered with kitty litter in the container for 30 minutes after the microwave finishes as the flowers will continue the drying process. Check your flowers for dryness and return to the microwave for another couple of minutes if need be.

Store dried flowers in an airtight container with a small amount of kitty litter to absorb any dampness.

2. Place 5 cm (2'') of silica gel in the bottom of a microwave-proof container then position the shortened flower stems down into this. Cover the flower heads carefully with more silica gel crystals. Place ½ cup of water in the oven with the container then put the oven on high for two to four minutes. When finished leave the flowers in the crystals overnight if possible. Store in an airtight container.

Freeze Drying

Freeze drying flowers and foliages is a relatively new innovation, although freeze drying other products has been around for some time. This unique process dry preserves 90% of all flowers, giving them an extended life period of 6–12 months. It is the best of all the drying methods for maintaining the fresh look of most living blooms and presents a wonderful way to preserve bridal bouquets and other keepsakes. However, it is less suitable for drying foliages; according to the machine manufacturer glycerining gives a softer and more successful result.

The practice of freeze drying changes the water in plant materials into ice crystals, then by a process of raising the temperature while at the same time lowering the atmospheric pressure, water is driven off the material's surface as vapour and extracted by a condensing process.

This is a simplification of a system which needs to be thoroughly studied in conjunction with the manufacturer's instructions. Be advised though, while these freeze dried flowers etc. are becoming widely popular in India, USA, Japan and now Australia, machine prices can range from $50,000–70,000 so this method is only suited to the commercially minded. For further information about machines, contact 'Freeze Tec' Newmarket, Auckland, New Zealand or 'Dynavac', Wantirna South, Victoria, Australia.

Pressed Flowers and Foliages

Whilst some pressed flowers and foliages can take on rather a stiff appearance, others like maidenhair fern, can look truly attractive.

Pressed flowers and foliages used in giftlines such as flower pictures, on greeting cards, in collages and the like make most appealing novelties.

Pressed flowers and foliages in picture frame

Choosing plant material for pressing

Flowers and foliages need to be pressed immediately after they have been picked, so have all your materials and tools ready.

As with other preservation techniques, always pick plants in their peak condition. Make sure they are clean and dry and blot away any dampness with blotting paper.

To achieve the greatest success with pressed flowers, choose flowers which are flat, single-petalled, thin-tissued and open. Single roses, single delphiniums, pansies, forget-me-nots, violets, boronias, kangaroo paws and many others make good subjects. Ferns, grasses and individual leaves provide the basis for interesting background material.

Flowers or foliages containing large amounts of water such as succulents are unsuitable, as are flowers with hard cores or rigid petals. Clusters of flowers can be separated from their stems, whilst large flowers can have their petals removed to be used individually. Any stalks used should be as thin as possible, and can be gently curved into shape with sticky tape. If you are using larger stalks, make sure they are soft enough to press.

How to press your flowers and foliages

Flower presses can be used but an inexpensive method of pressing flowers and foliages is to place them between the pages of a heavy book. That's where old telephone directories come into use. And the beauty is that if any staining of the pages occurs, it doesn't matter.

Firstly, lay the flowers and other plant material on a sheet of blotting or tissue paper. Make sure that none of the petals or pieces overlap or touch each other. If petals do overlap, slide a piece of tissue paper between the surfaces. To avoid handling and potentially damaging fragile material, arrange the pieces on the paper with the aid of a small paint or makeup brush. Cover with another piece of paper so the flowers etc. are sandwiched.

Place in the back pages of a book and work forward so as not to disturb previously placed layers. Cut tags and label the pages with the names of each flower or foliage being pressed, e.g. kangaroo paws, pansies, ferns, flannel flowers, etc. Have these tags so they extend from each section so the sections are identifiable at a glance.

Weight plays an important factor in the success of pressing flowers, so you may need to add more books to the top of the original pressing book.

If you are using a flower press tighten the wing nuts gently for the first 10 days or so. This allows the material to settle. Then tighten the nuts more securely during the following weeks.

Flowers can be pressed from anything as long as three months to a year. The longer the plant material is pressed the thinner it becomes, so the choice is up to you.

To avoid mould and to aid in the dehydration of the pressing plant material, make sure the procedure is taking place in a dry area.

To help retain the colour of pressed flowers and foliages, when the pressing time is up, remove them from the press, lift the top layer of paper and lightly sprinkle with borax powder. Cover them again with the sheet of paper and place in an airtight container, making sure to keep the plant materials flat. Store for another few weeks before using.

Pressing ferns using steam iron

Some ferns dry successfully by pressing with a hot iron, in particular maidenhair fern. Place the fern between two sheets of waxed paper (sandwich wrap) making sure the waxed side is lying against the fern. Fill an iron with water and set it on 'woollens' and cover the top layer of paper with a cloth to avoid burning the paper. Iron for up to five minutes, lifting the paper every so often to release any build-up of steam. The end result should be a shiny green fern which will retain its colour for a long period.

This method can also be used for other fine ferns such as *Sticherus* (umbrella fern) or *Bowenia serrulata* (Byfield fern).

Instead of wax paper, blotting paper can be used, but a change in colour may occur.

Getting Started

The following lists show the commonly used methods for preserving cut flowers and foliages and the species which would seem suitable for each method. Some plants have been included because of the successful preservation of similar types or species, even though their particular drying potential is unknown. No doubt you will soon wish to add your own plants to these lists.

Suggestions for air-drying

Acacia (wattle, esp. *A. macredenia*)
Achillea (yarrow)
Acrolinium (rose everlasting daisy)
Actinodium cunninghamii (Albany daisy)

Allium (garlic, leeks and onion flower heads)

Anigozanthos species (kangaroo paw)

Banksia species

Barley

Beaufortia decussata

Beaufortia sparsa

Celosia (cockscomb)

Chrysanthemum parthenium (button chrysanthemum)

Conospermum (smoke bush)

Craspedia (billy buttons)

Cytisus (broom)

Delphinium (larkspur)

Dillwynia retorta (eggs and bacon)

Dipsacus (teasel)

Dryandra praemorsa (cut-leaf dryandra)

Dryandra formosa (showy dryandra)

Eucalyptus species

Grevillea hookeriana

Grasses

Gypsophila esp. 'Bristol Fairy' (baby's breath)

Helichrysum species (everlasting daisy/paper daisy/strawflower)

Helipterum species (everlasting daisy/paper daisy)

Hydrangea

Hypocalymma puniceum

Isopogon species (drumsticks)

Ixodia achillioides (South Australian daisy)

Lachnostachys (lamb's tail)

Lavandula (lavender)

Leucadendron

Liatris (gay feather)

Limonium 'Misty' pink, white, blue

Limonium 'Oceanic' white, blue

Limonium sinuata (statice)

Lunaria annua (honesty)

Melaleuca heugelii

Melaleuca acuminata

Molucella laevis (Bells of Ireland)

Oats

Protea species

Ptilotus (mulla mulla incl. 'pussytails')

Roses (preferably in bud)

Rumex (dock)

Salix caprea (pussy willow)

Serruria florida ('Blushing Bride')

Serruria florida ('Sugar 'n Spice')

Solidago (golden rod)

Verticordia species

Waitzia acuminata (everlasting daisy)

Wheat

Suggestions for using desiccants

Actinotus helanthi, A. superbus (flannel flower)

Agapanthus (individual florets)

Blandfordia grandiflora (Christmas bells)

Bowenia serrulata (Byfield fern)

Brachycome iberidifolia (Swan River daisy)

Brunonia australis (blue pincushion)

Carnation

Castanospermum australe (black bean flowers)

Ceratopetalum gummiferum (NSW Christmas bush)

Clianthus formosa (Sturt's desert pea)

Cochlosperum gillivraei (kapok bush)

Crinum pedunculatum (river lily)

Dahlia varieties

Dampiera species

Dianthus

Eriostemon species (wax flower)

Freesia

Glossodia

Gompholobium

Hibbertia

Iris

Lechenaultia

Lilium longiflorum (Christmas lily)

Linum marginale

Marguerite (daisy)

Melastoma denticulatum

Narcissus (daffodils and jonquils)

Nigella (love-in-a-mist)

Orchids

Ornithogalum

Paeonia (paeony flower)

Rhododendron

Roses

Scabiosa (pincushion)

Sphaerolobium macranthus

Sweet peas

Tagetes (marigold)

Thysanotus multiflorus (fringed lily)
Tulip
Typhonium brownii (dark purple arum-like lily)
Violets
Xyris
Zantedeschia (calla lily)

Suggestions for Glycerining

Adiantum (maidenhair fern)
Aspidistra
Athertonia diversifolia (almond tree foliage)
Betula pendula (silver birch)
Brassaia actinophylla (umbrella tree foliage)
Daviesia cordata (book leaf)
Eucalyptus (esp. *E. cinerea* 'spinning gum')
Gladioli (foliage)
Grevillea (foliage)
Gypsophila (esp. 'Bristol Fairy')
Hedera (ivy)
Helichrysum diosmifolium (wild rice/sago bush)
Hydrangea
Iris (foliage)
Lauris nobilis (bay laurel)
Magnolia grandiflora (foliage)
Molucella laevis (Bells of Ireland)
Oreocallis wickhamii (North Queensland tree waratah foliage)
Pittosporum (diamond laurel)
Pteridium esculentum (bracken fern)
Solidago (golden rod)
Sticherus (umbrella fern)
Thryptomene calycina

Suggestions for pressing

Acacia (wattle)
Actinotus helianthi, *A. superbus* (flannel flower)

Actinodium cunninghamii (Albany daisy)
Adiantum (maidenhair fern)
Anigozanthos species (kangaroo paw)
Bauera rubioides (pink dog rose)
Bowenia serrulata (Byfield fern)
Brachycome species (Australian daisy)
Ceratopetalum gummiferum (NSW Christmas bush)
Clianthus formosa (Sturt's desert pea)
Dampiera species
Darwinia species
Daviesia cordata (book leaf)
Delphinium (larkspur)
Epacris species (common heath)
Eucalyptus
Gladioli (individual flowers)
Grasses
Hedera (ivy)
Helichrysum species (everlasting daisy/paper daisy/straw flower)
Helipterum species (everlasting daisy/paper daisy)
Hibbertia species
Iris
Lunaria annua (honesty)
Marguerite (daisy)
Melaleuca species
Monotoca species (individual bells)
Myosotis alpestria (forget-me-nots)
Paeonia (peony foliage)
Pansy
Papaver (poppies)
Patersonia sericea (native iris)
Pimelea linifolia 'Pink form' (button flower)
Pteridium esculentum (bracken fern)
Ptilotus species (mulla mulla incl. 'pussytails')
Sticherus (umbrella fern)
Violets
Waitza (everlasting daisy)

6 Bleaching and Dyeing Cut Flowers and Foliages

Bleaching

A process for the enthusiast to experiment with. Try bleaching wild oats, wheat, thistle, ferns, eucalyptus leaves, hydrangeas and other plants of your choice.

You will find some materials will need full strength bleach; others respond to a mixture of 50% bleach and 50% water. Bleaching time can take anywhere from 15 minutes to one day depending on the material you are bleaching. Over-bleaching can weaken petals, stems and foliage.

When the colour of the plant material has been bleached out, rinse material in cold water and hang up in an airy place to dry. Keep away from sunlight which may give the materials a yellowing effect. Scrupulous attention must be paid to removing all traces of bleach or sulphur dioxide if you intend to dye the bleached flowers or foliages.

Note: Bleaching is not a pre-requisite to dyeing. You may however need to bleach dark-coloured plant material if you wish to dye it to a lighter shade.

Canned Dyes

The fastest method of dyeing plant material, either living or dried, is by using aerosol canned dyes. One brand available is 'Designmaster', sold through florist suppliers and some flower markets.

The colour range of canned dyes is huge and the finished effect is most attractive. Colours can be mixed when damp to give an even wider colour range. Pre-dyed light colours can be dyed over with darker colours. Drying time for dyed materials is about 10–15 minutes.

When using these products avoid inhalation of the dye as well as skin contact in case of toxicity.

Textile Dyes

The most commonly dyed plant materials are dried wildflowers, foliages and grasses. Dyes used are usually those designed for textiles. In the past food dyes have been used and although food dyes are relatively safe to handle, the range of colours can be limited and they aren't always lightfast. They are also more expensive than other dyes because of the costly toxicity testing required for food additives.

Out of the textile dye range, those dyes designed for dyeing acrylic fibres tend to give the best results. These are known as 'basic dyes'. Small amounts can be purchased at most chemists in a wide range of colours. For commercial dyers 5 kg lots and over can be purchased through chemical companies like Ciba-Geigy in Melbourne.

Follow manufacturer's directions regarding the water to dye ratio. Gloves and dust masks should be worn when weighing out the powder. If possible, the water should be boiling. Use a large tub or bath. Stir the dye throughout the dyeing process to maintain an evenness of colour. Dip the plant material in the dye solution. Using rubber gloves squeeze out excess solution. Stand plant material upright in plastic buckets or other non-corrosive containers to dry or on plastic meshing in airy surrounds, but out of direct sunlight which will fade the dye. To avoid colour contamination make sure that different plant materials and colours aren't touching.

Absorption Dyes

This form of dyeing means that the living plant material is stood in the dye solution. As the plant drinks, it absorbs the dye and becomes coloured. Mostly used for light-coloured plants, this method can also be used to highlight veins in darker plant material using bright coloured dyes like red.

Many absorption dyes can be added to glycerine solution used to dry plant material. As the flowers or foliage dry, they also become dyed!

Absorption dyeing is a trial and error procedure since some plant species do not give good colouring results. For the best effect use freshly picked, good quality flowers or foliages which have a fast water usage rate. Re-cut stems on an angle under water before placing in the dye solution. This removes any air blockages and means the plant stems won't be sitting flat on the base of the container.

Follow manufacturer's directions. Warm dye solution is absorbed into the stems more readily than cold so heat the solution to between 30° and 40°C before placing stems into it.

The best results are generally obtained with food dyes although cotton dyes can be used. One supplier is the company Robert Bryce in Melbourne.

7 Tips For Potential Commercial Growers

What Should I Grow?

You may have a wonderful idea or a particular preference for a certain flower or foliage but it may not be what the market place is asking for. So how do you find out what it is you should be growing?

Before embarking on a growing project you will have to turn yourself into a detective. Find out where the local flower markets are and make appointments to see the managers. Ask them what plant materials are most sought-after. What prices are being fetched—that is, what price could you expect to be paid and what is the wholesale price? Is the market policy C.O.D. to you or would you need to issue an invoice? Remember it is up to you to determine how long you are prepared to wait for your money. Many markets operate on a 7-day account with their customers.

Find out how much of the plant material you would need to supply in one delivery and how many deliveries would be expected of you in one year. What time of the day are deliveries expected to arrive? Find out if there are any other local growers of that plant material or if it comes from out of the area. Which colours are the most popular and how long do you need to grow the stems? What is the expected vase life, i.e. how many days is the plant material expected to live? What type of packaging is required for delivery or could you deliver fresh material in buckets? Does the required plant material dry and if so, does the market already buy enough dried material, or could you supply that too?

You may need to go outside your local area. By interviewing market managers in areas with different climates you may find that you can supply 'off season' flowers or foliages.

Next visit florists in the geographical areas you wish to supply. What are their requirements? Do they want the same plant material suggested by the flower market? Ask them some of the same questions you asked the flower markets. What stem length do they want on their plant material? How many stems per bunch? What vase life is desirable?

Do they want their plant material sleeved? Do they buy direct from growers and if so, what are they paying now for their plant material? How many suppliers have they got for that species? You may have to supply something else if there is too much competition.

How often would they expect delivery in the week and at what time of day? Do they have peak periods like Mother's Day or Valentine's Day for that particular plant material? If so, by what percentage could you expect your orders to increase? Interview as many florists as possible. Find out if there are any florist associations or major floral art schools in the vicinity.

Now that you have some idea of what you should be growing, take a trip to your local Department of Agriculture. See if they have any growing information on your potential crop, both written and verbal. Are there any pests and diseases about which you should be aware? Should that crop be grown out in the open or under cover? What about irrigation, soil types and windbreaks? Does the crop need to be supported by wire or stakes? How long after planting could you start harvesting?

Many growers' groups are formed with the help of the Department of Agriculture—ask them if they know of any groups you could join. Attend the meetings as they often have guest speakers who will keep you in touch with what is happening in the industry. See if the Department of Agriculture has any newsletters from these groups, or if there are any scheduled day trips to cut flower farms.

Trends

The cut flower industry is forever increasing and becoming more competitive, not only on a national basis but also internationally. If you are serious about becoming a flower grower you will need to keep up to date with the latest trends.

One way of doing this is to do a lot of reading. There are several excellent industry journals to which you can subscribe. *The Flower Link*, Windsor Road, Northmead, is a free monthly magazine and about one of the best. *Australian Horticulture*, available from newsagents or by subscription, frequently features articles on the industry. You may wish to become an associate member of Interflora and Teleflora so you can receive their magazines, again to see actually how flowers and foliages are used in the trade. One of the best magazines for following overseas trends is the U.S. based *The Florist*. It pays to find out what is being used elsewhere in the world as Australia is often in line for the same product.

Keep in touch with your local Department of Agriculture. They have divisions dealing specifically with the cut flower industry and often send their representatives overseas to investigate the major worldwide flower markets like the flower auctions in Aalsmeer (Holland) as well as overseas cut flower farms.

Find out about the major cut flower shows in and outside your area and attend as many as

possible to see how flowers and foliages are being used. The Society for Growing Australian Plants (S.G.A.P.) often hold exciting native plant exhibitions and then there is Australia's major flower show—The Australian National Flower Show—started in 1989 in Melbourne. Exhibitors attend from all over Australia and the show is truly fantastic.

Marketing

Don't be put off by the term. It's just another word for selling. And how do you sell your flowers and foliages? As fresh as possible and in the best physical condition! Don't be tempted to add that inferior flower stem to your bunch—nothing will destroy your credibility more.

As you would have found out from your investigations, when it comes to bunching flowers etc. there are some standard practices. Roses, gladioli, sim carnations and sprays are normally sold 10 stems to a bunch. Chrysanthemums are sold with 8-15 stems per bunch, while lilies, Singapore orchids and hyacinths are sold with 5 stems to the bunch. Banksias and proteas are sold either 5 to the bunch or individually. Gypsophila and limonium (statice) are often sold by weight. But there are no hard and fast rules for most other flowers and foliages—a lot depends on what you, the grower, supply. So once again, it's a good idea to have a look at a few flower markets and gauge the average size of bunches.

Stems are normally tied together by elastic bands. If the flower heads are heavy or delicate like sim carnations, sometimes two bands are needed, one at the base of the stems and one close to the flower heads for support.

Plant material for floral arrangements comes in four major categories:

1. Focal flowers are the flowers which draw the eye in an arrangement. These are usually large, striking or expensive, e.g. proteas, gerberas and roses.

2. Secondary flowers are used as an accompaniment to the focals, e.g. spray carnations and daffodils.

3. Filler flowers are used to soften and 'fill' the arrangement, e.g. thryptomene, statice and gypsophila.

4. Foliages, ferns and grasses are used to add texture and greenery to an arrangement.

Again the rules are flexible depending upon the size of the arrangement. For instance in a small arrangement sometimes the secondary flowers can become the focal point!

Consistency of supply and continuity of quality are both important factors in marketing flowers. As a supplier, there is always somebody ready to jump into your spot so it's important to build up a good working relationship with your customers. Always try to deliver your products at the same time of day and week. Customers tend to keep a look out for you and regularity makes for good relationships.

Keep your pricing right—that is, don't undercut the market. This is where being a member of a growers' group will help you to keep informed about reasonable prices. The cut flower industry is a professional business and there is an accepted level of prices. You do yourself and the industry as a whole no good if you give your product away. If you are selling direct to florists check regularly with the markets to see what the current wholesale price is. Buying direct from you, the grower, is already saving the florist money by not having to telephone through an order or pay freight and packing costs. You must watch your overheads and take into account the money spent on petrol as well as the time it takes making your delivery. Also make sure accounts are paid to you on time. Bad debts are a quick way to go out of business.

As a service to your flower market or florist you may wish to write name-tags on new lines or unusual plant materials, using both the botanical and common names. This way everyone becomes familiar with the product. If you sleeve your flowers you may also like to label the sleeves with your company name.

Transporting Cut Flowers and Foliage

The method of transport you use will depend largely on whether you are making personal deliveries or freighting your product. If making personal deliveries, many growers have their vans fitted out with racks along the sides into which they can slip buckets. This way flowers and foliages can be placed in a holding solution (see chapter 'Cutting and Storing Flowers and Foliages' for solution formula) and the flowers and foliages stay fresh as the growers make their rounds. Some growers park their vans outside the florist shops and the florists go to the van to choose what they want. In other cases the grower simply picks out the ordered, bucketed plant material and takes it into the florist or flower market.

If you are freighting your product to the consumer, be it market place or florist, you will need a strong box. At this stage there isn't a standard flower box. There are chrysanthemum boxes, carnation boxes and an odd assortment of other boxes. To find out what is best for your own needs contact a large packaging company and find out what boxes are available specifically for the transportation of cut flowers.

When using boxes you will have to pay attention to the packing methods you employ to ensure minimal crushing of flowers. It is usual to pack heavy flowers like proteas on the bottom and work your way up through the box using lighter and more delicate plant material.

Proteas and banksias aren't normally wrapped but most other flowers and foliages are. This not only protects them but also holds in the size of the bunch, acting as a space saving measure. The heads of flowers are always covered and the bunches are wrapped firmly but not tightly. Butcher's paper is commonly used and once wrapped, the plant material is packed in the box with the stems facing in towards the centre. The box is then taped securely and labelled.

Do not overfill or underfill boxes with flowers

etc. as this will only lead to product damage. Packing a flower box is a real art!

Where possible try to secure the return of your carton, otherwise add a small packing and carton charge to your invoice. Cartons are expensive items.

Exporting

So you want to export your cut flowers or foliages! Normally to do so means you will have already established a good home market and exporting will be an extension of this; or you may decide to grow just for the export market.

There are several ways to go about exporting. You may wish to go it alone, finding your own overseas market and handling all the freighting and selling yourself; or you may belong to a growers' group and decide to pool your resources and export in larger quantities; or you may decide to enlist the aid of an export agent.

The best way to decide which way you want to choose is to do some research. Firstly, the Department of Primary Industries or the Department of Agriculture are worth speaking to. They can often help by giving you an idea of how other growers have gone about the export process. Sometimes they have information about the export of specific crops; other times the information will be more general.

Then there is Austrade—the Australian Trade Commission. Again, they often have details about cut flowers and foliage crops and overseas markets. Austrade have a number of divisions dealing with all aspects of export and will be able to help you right from the basics of custom tariff requirements, quarantine information, etc. through to information on what overseas markets look for in cut flower and foliage products. Some of the information must be paid for although they do present an interesting Exporter's Kit free of charge.

It's also a good idea to speak to a few different cut flower agents before you get into the export field. Be frank with them and tell them you are thinking of exporting. Mention what you are growing and ask their advice on your marketing strategy.

If, as a grower, you are going to export through your own means, you will need to produce a product that is of the highest standard. Whatever crop you have chosen to export will normally need to be far superior in quality to that required for sale on the homefront. For example, proteas, banksias, etc. must have completely straight stems, whereas at home this is not necessary. There must be no sign of pests or diseases. You will need to know how many stems to pack to a box. Some countries have strict computer systems and work in rigid units. They do not appreciae a grower 'throwing' in an extra stem for good measure.

Again, this is where your market research skills must be used. You need to know every facet of how the market you are selling to operates. You need to know what their import requirements are and what documentation is required to accompany your product. First find out in Australia what is needed but also have someone in your overseas market place double check for you. This is particularly important when sending products to non-English speaking countries where details may be lost in the translation.

The Australian Quarantine Inspection Service have to inspect your export cargo and issue a Phytosanitary Certificate, i.e. a plant health certificate to state that your cut flower or foliage shipment is free from pests and disease. You will need to pay for this service. The checks are random and done per sq. root, i.e. if you have 100 boxes they will check 10.

Product research for your proposed market must be thorough. Countries have their idiosyncracies. For instance, Japan doesn't like black edged flowers. To them black is a colour signifying mourning and they don't particularly like 'fringed' flowers either.

It may be far more beneficial for you as a grower to use an export agent. Agents' names are listed in the telephone book. In some cases agents can be recommended by the Department of Primary Industry or Department of Agriculture, cut flower markets or even by some airlines.

Agents usually work in one of two ways. Either you sell your product direct to them for a fixed price and they then take care of the overseas marketing or you give your product to the agent on consignment. In either case small quantities can be added to other growers' shipments by the agent, giving the small producer a chance to export. If on consignment, airway charges like Airport Tax, Freight and Consignment Note costs are normally taken out of your nett remittance when your goods are sold. Agents usually pay you monthly and can take anywhere between 10%–17½% out of your nett remittance as their fee.

Having an agent can take a lot of worry out of the export industry as they are the ones keeping an eye on overseas market trends and prices and can keep you well informed as to what product is required.

Don't forget, whether you go it alone or whether you choose an agent, you will have to get your product to either the airport or to the agent. Will you drive it there yourself or will you use refrigerated freighters? Think of the costs and put it together with all your other costs. Can you afford to export? Can you keep up consistency of quality and quantity? Can you supply what the overseas market place wants? Cut flowers and foliages are judged on their appearance and how long they last. So post harvest care, i.e. conditioning and careful packaging to avoid crushing petals and leaves, is of ultimate importance.

Exporting cut flowers and foliages can have its rewards but careful planning is required. For example, in the summer months of the Northern Hemisphere there is an overabundance of flowers. So plan your flowers for their off-season. Play the market. Australian native flowers could be another opening in the overseas market. The market place is always looking for the unusual, and according to the October 1992 issue of the *Austrade Exporter*, Japan is the largest export market for Australian native flowers.

These are only guidelines for when it all boils down, no-one can tell you what to grow and export. It is through your own research that your choices must be made.

General Index

Common Names

Acorn banksia *see Banksia prionotes*
Albany daisy *see Actinodium cunninghamii*
Annual statice *see Limonium*
Anthurium lily *see Anthurium andreanum*
Basket flower *see Adenanthos obovata*
Bay laurel *see Lauris nobilis*
Bell flower *see Geleznowia verrucosa*
Bells of Ireland *see Molucella laevis*
Billy buttons *see Craspedia*
Bird's nest banksia *see Banksia baxteri*
Bird's nest fern *see Asplenium nidus*
Black stemmed maidenhair *see Adiantum formosum*
Blue almond tree *see Athertonia diversifolia*
Blue lechenaultia *see Lechenaultia biloba*
Blushing Bride *see Serruria florida*
Bookleaf *see Daviesia cordata*
Boston fern *see Nephrolepis exalata*
Box *see Buxus*
Broom *see Genista*
Brown boronia *see Boronia megastigma*
Browneii *see Verticordia*
Burdett's banksia *see Banksia burdetti*
Byfield fern *see Bowenia serrulata*
Carnation *see Dianthus caryophyllus*
Candytuft *see Iberis*
Calla lily *see Zantedeschia*
Cauli Morrison *see Verticordia*
Cape York lily *see Curcuma australasica*
Christmas bells *see Blandfordia grandiflora or B. punicea*
Christmas lily *see Lilium longiflorum*
Coarse tassel fern *see Lycopodium phlegmaria*
Cockscomb *see Celosia*
Common heath *see Epacris impressa*
Common tassel fern *see Lycopodium phlegmaria*
Cooktown orchid *see Dendrobium bigibbum 'Superbum'*
Cornflower *see Centaurea cyanis*
Corn lily *see Ixia*
Cottonbush *see Pimelea nivea*
Croton *see Codiae variegatum*
Cut-leaved dryandra *see Dryandra praemorsa*
Daffodil *see Narcissus*
Dolly bush *see Cassinia aculeata*
Donkey orchid *see Diuris longifolia*
Drumsticks *see Isopogon dubius*
Dune pine *see Callitris rhomboidea*
Dwarf bamboo *see Sasa fortunei*
Easter daisy *see Aster novi-belgi*
Emu grass *see Podocarpus drydougana*
Ermine tail protea *see Protea longifolia*
Esperance wax *see Chamelaucium axillare*.
Evergreen magnolia *see Magnolia grandiflora*
Everlasting daisy *see Helichrysum or Helipterum*
Fairy-bells orchid *see Sarcochilius ceciliae*
Forget-me-not *see Myosotis alpestria*
Foxglove *see Digitalis*
Foxtail fern *see Asparagus densiflorus*
Fringed lily *see Thysanotus multiflorus*
Gay feather *see Liatris spicata*
Geraldton wax *see Chamelaucium uncinatum*
Giant maidenhair *see Adiantum formosum*
Gladioli *see Gladiolus*
Glory wattle *see Acacia spectabilis*
Golden flowering banksia *see Banksia media*

Golden nitens *see Verticordia*
Grass tree *see Xanthorrhoea*
Gungurru gum *see Eucalyptus caesia*
Heath *see Erica* or *Epacris impressa*
Heath leaf banksia *see Banksia ericifolia*
Hill Banksia *see Banksia spinulosa*
Honesty *see Lunaria annua*
Honey protea *see Protea repens*
Honeysuckle banksia *see Banksia marginata*
Hooker's banksia *see Banksia hookeriana*
Hop bush *see Dodonea pinnata* and *D. triquetra*
Iceland poppy *see Papaver*
Illyarrie gum *see Eucalyptus erythrocorys*
Jonquil *see Narcissus*
Kangaroo paw *see Anigozanthos*
King protea *see Protea cynaroides*
Kruse's mallee *see Eucalyptus kruseana*
Large-fruited mallee *see Eucalyptus youngiana*
Larkspur *see Delphinium*
Lamb's tails *see Lachnostachys eriobotrya*
Lavender *see Lavandula*
Leather leaf fern *see Rumohra adiantiformis*
Lemon-scented ti-tree *see Leptospermum petersonii*
Lilac bells *see Tetratheca pilosa*
Lisianthus *see Eustoma russelliana*
Long club moss *see Lycopodium myrtifolium*
Maidenhair fern *see Adiantum capillus veneris*
Marigold *see Tagetes*
Menzies' banksia *see Banksia menziesii*
Michaelmas daisy *see Aster novi-belgi*
Misty Blue, pink, white *see Limonium*
Mountain bell *see Darwinia leiostyla*
Mountain daisy *see Ixodia achillioides*
Mountain moss *see Lycopodium myrtifolium*
Mottlecah gum *see Eucalyptus macrocarpa*
Mourning bride *see Scabiosa atropurpurea*
Mulla mulla *see Ptilotus exaltatus*
Narrow-leaf cone bush *see Petrophile linearis*
Native daisy *see Olearia tomentosa*
Native Iris *see Patersonia sericea*
Native rose *see Boronia serrulata*
'Neri' *see Protea nerifolia*
New Zealand flax *see Phormium*
NSW Christmas bush *see Ceratopetalum gummiferum*
Nth Qld tree waratah *see Oreocallis wickhamii*
November lily *see Lilium longiflorum*
Oceanic blue *see Limonium*
Old maid's pincushion *see Scabiosa atropurpurea*
Orange blossom orchid *see Sarcochilius falcatus*
Orange fluted gum *see Eucalyptus pterocarpa*
Paeony rose *see Paeonia officinalis*
Paper daisy *see Helipterum*
Parrot pea *see Dillwynia floribunda*
Perennial aster *see Aster novi-belgi*
Perennial phlox *see Phlox paniculata*
Perennial scabiosa *see Scabiosa caucasica*
Peruvian lily *see Alstroemeria*
Pincushion flower *see Scabiosa caucasica*
Pincushion hakea *see Hakea laurina*
Pincushion protea *see Leucospermum*
Pineapple lily *see Eucomis comosa*
Pink boronia *see Boronia pilosa*
Pink dog rose *see Baurea rubioides*
Pink mink protea *see Protea nerifolia*

Pink star leucospermum *see Leucospermum tottum*
Port Jackson pine *see Callitris rhomboidea*
Pouched coral fern *see Gleichenia dicarpa*
Prince protea *see Protea compacta*
Pussy willow *see Salix caprea*
Queen Anne's lace *see Ammi majus*
Queensland silver wattle *see Acacia podalyriifolia*
Queen protea *see Protea magnifica*
Ravine orchid *see Sarcochilius fitzgeraldii*
Red boronia *see Boronia heterophylla*
Red flowering gum *see Eucalyptus ficifolia*
River lily *see Crinum pedunculatum*
River peppermint gum *see Eucalyptus elata*
Rose *see Rosa*
Rose cockade *see Leucadendron tinctum*
Rose mallee *see Eucalpytus rhodantha*
Scarlet Banksia *see Banksia coccinea*
Scorpion everlasting daisy *see Helichrysum scorpioides*
Scrub leaves *see Ptostrata*
Showy banksia *see Banksia speciosa*
Showy dog rose *see Bauera sessiliflora*
Showy dryandra *see Dryandra formosa*
Singapore orchid *see Dendrobium*
Silver birth *see Betula pendula*
Silver-leafed mountain gum *see Eucalyptus pulverulenta*
Silver dollar gum *see Eucalyptus cinerea*
Silver wattle *see Acacia dealbata*
Smoke bush *see Conospermum*
Snapdragon *see Antirrhinum*
Sth Australian daisy *see Exodia achillioides*
Stock *see Matthiola*
Strawflower *see Helichrysum*
Square-fruited mallee *see Eucalyptus tetraptera*
Sturt's desert pea *see Clianthus formosa*
'Sugar n' Spice' *see Serruria florida*
Swan River myrtle *see Hypocalymma robustum*
Swamp banksia *see Banksia robur*
Swamp bloodwood *see Eucalpytus ptychocarpa*
Sweet pea *see Lathyrus odoratus*
Sweet scabious *see Scabiosa atropurpurea*
Tallerack gum *see Eucalyptus tetragona*
Tasmanian blue gum *see Eucalyptus globulus*
Tasmanian daisy bush *see Olearia stellulata*
Throatwort *see Trachelium*
Tortured willow *see Salix matsudana*
Tuberose *see Polianthes tuberosa*
Tulip *see Tulipa*
Umbrella fern *see Sticherus*
Umbrella treesee *Brassaia actinophylla*
Violets *see Viola*
Waratah *see Telopea speciosissima or T. truncata*
Water lily *see Nymphea filifolia*
Wattle *see Acacia*
Waxflower *see Eriostemon*
Wedding bush *see Ricinocarpus tuberculatus*
Weeping Brisbane wattle *see Acacia perangusta*
White-leaved marlock *see Eucalyptus tetragona*
Willow peppermint *see Eucalyptus nicholii*
Woolly foxglove *see Pityrodia axillaris*
Woody pear *see Xylomelum pyriforme or X. angustifolium*
Yarrow *see Achillea*
Yellow tulip *see Leucadendron laureolum*
Zig zag wattle *see Acacia macredenia*

Botanical Names